MILLION DOLLAR Salespeople

by Lisa Coleman

Published By:

Scrivo, Inc.

7904 E. Chaparral Road, Suite A110-223

Scottsdale AZ 85250

FAX (602) 945-2603

ISBN 0-9660493-0-6

Second Edition revised, 1998

This book is dedicated to the memory of

Walter N. Hunter

Million Dollar Salespeople:

Success Stories of Top Sales Performers

INTRODUCTION

It has been said that the will to persevere in the face of obstacles is often the difference between success and failure. American inventor Charles F. Kettering said that "virtually nothing comes out right the first time. Failures, repeated failures, are posts on the road to achievement." Capitalism in our society is an achievement within itself and has evolved to its present state through trial and error, failures and successes. Free enterprise has persevered. It is organized as a market, so buying and selling have to work hand in hand for our economy to succeed. Consequently, the producer has a right to make what he wants and the consumer has a right to choose what he wants buy.... hence the transaction. But the transaction generally doesn't take place without a necessary link, THE necessary link, the strongest in the chain.... the salesperson.

This book examines a diverse group of salespeople representing different kinds of businesses. They speak candidly about everything from prior jobs and educational backgrounds, to sales figures, achievements, and personal philosophies. These are the best of the best.

These highly skilled sales performers are exceptional people, not because of their incomes, but because of their unique style and integrity. By learning what makes each of them who they are, a better understanding will be gained of what it takes to really succeed in sales. Who they are today, and what they have achieved, is a direct result of what they have experienced along the way—where they grew up, their first jobs, their parents, their values, their hobbies, and the things in their lives that have nothing directly to do with their profession. They are molded, like we all are, by life. These chapters focus primarily on the road to success rather than success itself, and enhance the testimony that there isn't any goal that cannot be reached if the desire is strong enough.

The result of selling is money. Billions and billions of dollars change hands every day through sales of some sort. Most business people have a great deal of respect for the proverbial "salesperson" and what he or she does. There is a definite respect owed to those who have the ability to sell. And there is truly a certain gift that enables one to tolerate the constant rejection, the seemingly endless hours, and the inevitable stigma that comes with being labeled a "salesperson." Yet it is important to remember that without the salesperson, his or her drive, perseverance, and undaunted belief in a product, tangible or intangible, the sale will simply not take place, and business as we know it ceases to exist.

It would be safe to say that almost every successful businessperson has some kind of roots in sales. Tire and rubber mogul Harvey Firestone started his career as a carriage salesman. He became very successful and soon saw the possibilities in manufacturing rubber carriage tires. Firestone began his own tire company in Chicago and sold it in 1899. The money earned from this sale enabled him to establish the Firestone Tire and Rubber Company in Akron, Ohio. His first factory had only 12 workers, but he used his sales skills to acquire a large order from Henry Ford which helped launch his product and eventually made his name synonymous with tires in all areas of the auto industry. In more recent history, presidential hopeful and businessman Ross Perot began his career in sales. After his service in the U.S. Navy, he became a salesman for IBM. Perot worked for the company from 1957 to 1962 learning all he could about sales and the industry itself. He then formed his own company, Electronic Data Services (EDS), and within a decade, Ross Perot became a billionaire.

There are literally thousands of success stories just like these, and if you look closely, you will discover that being a salesperson is a very strong common denominator. When I was first approached about a book on "million dollar salespeople," I had these kinds of successes in mind. It seemed that there were plenty of books available about owners and high level executives of major corporations, but very few that focused on the true backbone of these magnates... the salespeople. The ones who have no ownership in their companies, the ones who aren't related to the boss, and the ones who really deserve a great deal of the credit for the successes of the businesses they are in. Salespeople whose names you probably don't know, but nonetheless have started at the ground level and worked their way to the top. Men and women who know the fears of having their financial future hang in the balance every time they pick up the phone, and the exaltation of closing a huge sale when they are working solely for commissions. The goal was to take a closer and more in-depth look at these number one sales performers and learn what makes them who they are, both personally and professionally.

As the research began, it became clear that most successful salespeople in this country, some making enormous amounts of money, are essentially the same as everyone else. It was surprising, yet comforting, to find that some of our nation's finest and most successful salespeople were at one time a stand-up comedian, a dental hygienist, a stocker at a grocery store, a musician, a ski bum, a professional athlete, a waitress, a health spa membership seller, and a confused student. None of these salespeople were born into their success. They are all self-made examples of what it takes to work your way to the top. They have as many differences as they do similarities, and prove again and again that there is no set pattern to achieving success. It didn't take wealth and an affluent background, knowing the right people, or even an education (in some cases) for these salespeople to succeed. But it did take a combination of motivation, courage, and a relentless pursuit of wanting to be the very best. Tempered with a little good luck, when all is said and done, the common thread is hard work. Hard work doesn't cost any money, it doesn't require experience and it is something we all have the capacity to do.

More often than not, salespeople are driven by the almighty dollar, and the subjects of this book are no exception. Nonetheless, they have reached a level of success that has allowed them to reflect on what is and is not important to them. They all admit that money was the initial driving force, but as the money began to flow, they discovered that there was indeed much more to the entire process. It doesn't appear to be necessarily what these people sell, but rather who they are when they sell it. And the message seems altogether too simple: "Do what you love to do, do it well, and the money will follow." The sales figures for this special group are staggering, and financially they exceed most people's dreams. But when push comes to shove, they are just ordinary people who found a way to make it happen, and make it happen in a big way.

Who's who

Chapter 1: The Ski Bum

After hauling cement, painting houses and working the night shift at a warehouse, radio advertising sales was a big challenge. But he jumped in, moved up, and proved that little things can become very big things. Paul Leonard is the best and the brightest at Star Media Group in Dallas, Texas. His company specializes in the buying and selling of radio stations, and Paul's contributions have helped propel Star Media into the stratosphere of radio brokerage firms. Paul's transactional sales volume began at $58.5 million in 1992, and has kept moving decisively up... $82.75 million, $135 million, $235.25 million and over a billion from there.

Chapter 2: The Introvert

Quiet and shy, this stock boy was destined for grocery store management. But opportunity knocked, and he took the chance. Mike Pexa is one of the top agents in the country for Farmers Insurance Group. Based in Sacramento, California, he was named Agent of the Year for two consecutive years. He has been selected to the Presidents Council nine times, a group comprised of less than one percent of the entire 13,000 person agency force. He has broken all company records by writing over 10,000 policies in his career.

Chapter 3: The All-American Girl

Blonde, bright, and full of smiles and energy, waiting tables wasn't such a bad living. Well, not until someone mentioned the word "sales." Karen Vachon started on the ground floor as a confectionery salesperson with American Chicle, a division of Warner-

Lambert. Focusing on chewing gum and candy, Karen went from being a Retail Sales Representative stocking displays for minimum wage to the company's President Club Award Winner for top sales. Her sales averaged an impressive $25 million annually. (Karen took a brief career hiatus and is now a salesperson for an aluminum extrusion company.)

Chapter 4: The Teacher

He thought playing the drums was his ticket to success, but fortunately fate intervened, and the music played a bit more quietly. Scott Magnesen, based in Oakbrook, Illinois, is a Senior Vice President, and one of Dean Witter Reynolds Inc.'s top retail brokers. At 28 he was the youngest broker in Dean Witter's history to make their prestigious Chairman's Club. His gross commissions have grown 1700% since his first year as a broker. Scott has a client base of several thousand people and personally manages more than half a billion dollars worth of investments.

Chapter 5: The Die Hard

This dental hygienist wasn't overly thrilled with the prospect of multilevel marketing, but her engagement had fallen through, she was desperate, broke and willing to try anything. Anything turned out to be quite something. Leslie Stanford is among the top 5 producers in the world for Herbalife International. Based in Denver, Colorado, she has built a market share that brings her residual income from distributors in 27 different countries. Responsible for expanding Herbalife's North American territory into Canada, Leslie was a millionaire at the age of 27. Her monthly income surpasses $100,000, and the numbers keep increasing.

Chapter 6: The Psychologist

Moving to a new city and finding a career was not going to be easy, but the health spa industry was beginning to boom, and selling memberships might lead to some bigger things. As it turned out, much bigger things. Mark Moskowitz is the definitive example of a successful residential real estate broker. Working for Realty Executives in Phoenix, Arizona, Mark has shattered records and set new precedents in the real estate field. In 1992 he was named the top agent for Realty Executives in both the state of Arizona and the nation. In 1993, he was again named top agent in Arizona and finished second in the nation. The year 1994 again brought top honors from the state, as well as being named the number one agent in the United States, Canada, and Mexico, and the achievement awards continue. Mark's personal annual sales figures are edging $30 million.

Chapter 7: The Comedian

Juggling on a street corner and playing the comedy club circuit in New York wasn't going to pay the bills. Without a college degree things didn't look promising, but a fire and a good suggestion changed all that. Alan Fendrick, now a modern day entreprenuer with his own company, worked for Dataflex Corporation which was based in Edison, New Jersey. His primary focus was to sell computer hardware and services to Fortune 500 companies. Alan sold a record $30 million in hardware, and maintained an average of $15 million in sales for the first 7 years of his career. He later expanded his endeavors to include the selling of services, and in that area alone, recorded $5 million in sales a year against an industry average of $600 thousand.

Chapter 8: The Specialist

Winning was everything to this gifted athlete, but it seems his energies were better used hitting home runs in commercial real estate than at the ballpark. Jim Richardson was a First Vice President in the Biosciences Group of CB Commercial in Redwood City, California. (Jim has since made a transition within the industry and has become a senior officer at Alexandria Real Estate Equities.) CB Commercial is the largest commercial real estate company in the world, and Jim was instrumental in developing the biosciences division into a major money maker. He consistently ranked among the top producers of more than 2,000 commercial brokers, and was the driving force in evolving a three-person sales team into an 18-office, nationwide 25-person sales powerhouse. Jim's group brought in a combined total of over $200 million in transactional volume for CB Commercial, and his personal annual sales volume exceeded $50 million. He worked on a straight commission basis.

Chapter 9: The Rising Star

Uncertain in college as to a major, veterinary school appeared the way to go. Unfortunately, her college didn't provide the right curriculum and she was forced to make another choice—business. Diane Donley is the superstar at North America's second-largest printing company, Quebecor Printing. A subsidiary of the Montreal-based conglomerate, Diane's office is based in Boston, Massachusetts. At only 26 years of age, she had personally generated staggering sales figures ranging from over $6 million when she began in 1992, to a whopping $25 million in 1995. She was recognized as Salesperson of the Year in 1994 and continues to blaze a paper trail through the printing world.

THE SKI BUM

"Perfect discipline requires recognition of infallibility. Infallibility requires the observance of discipline."

George F. Kennan
American Diplomacy (1951)

The Ski Bum

Freshly fallen snow rises into the air in huge swirls of white powder as the blades of the helicopter begin to rotate. Flying high over the Colorado Rocky Mountains, skiers gaze out the windows in anticipation. As the elevation increases they know they are on the brink of a moment they will never forget. The pilot finds a pristine blanket of white on the mountaintop and sets down. In moments, the sound of their transport fades away and they find themselves alone at the pinnacle of a perfect wintery world. Miles of untracked glory await them as they check their equipment and make their way to the edge. This is every skier's dream, this is Paul Leonard's reality. And though he is no stranger to hard work, his passion is to play.

There are a thousand slopes Paul Leonard would like to ski, and with his sales figures reaching into the hundreds of millions, there is a fair chance he could reach them all. But until he breaks away for his next trip, Paul is content to be the top salesman for Star Media Group in the high stakes game of radio station brokerage. When buying and selling radio stations, the deals range in price anywhere from $5 million to $100 million on any given transaction, and it takes a relentless combination of intelligence and guts to keep up with the key players. Paul has made himself an expert at this game and likes how it feels to hold the best cards in the deck.

The fax I received from Paul confirming our meeting in Dallas said, "I will look for you at 7:00 A.M. sharp." I had deduced from our phone conversations, though light and funny, that when it came to business, Paul was just that. I arrived early to find his office still dark. At 7:00 A.M. straight up, I tried again—still dark. At 7:05 A.M. the lights went on and I found myself face to face with someone who appeared to be on his way to a luau rather than a meeting. Casual and confident, Paul glanced at his watch, laughed, and called me an "overachiever." We were friends instantly.

Born in Denver, Colorado, but making stops in North Dakota, Indiana, Missouri, California, and Washington throughout his childhood, Paul was a "retail brat." His father worked for J.C. Penney during the department store boom, so the family moved every couple of years to follow the new opportunities that became available with the company's progress. Paul has an incredible amount of respect for his father and how he was raised. "My father came from very, very simple beginnings, he barely graduated high-school, but he always knew how to work." Paul understood his father's career choice and didn't find it overly difficult to move from state to state. He did, however, find it to be rather traumatic always having to be "the new kid in school."

As the "new kid," Paul learned quickly to adapt to people and situations. It was a constant struggle to transcend from being the "low person on the totem pole in every strata," to somehow being accepted. His tools were his humor combined with an uncanny knack to read people. Even as a youngster, Paul prided himself in having the ability to sense people's motivations, not necessarily in a manipulative manner, but in a way that allowed him to influence people. Later in life this sense would help him open some doors he may not have otherwise been able to get through. Paul believes that moving around so much also forced him to develop a certain "competitive spirit" in order to survive amongst the pressures of new schools, new people and new situations. This is a "spirit" he has carried throughout his sales career and his life.

After attending a long list of public high schools, Paul found himself as a student at the University of Washington in Seattle. Not really certain what he wanted from life, Paul passed some time "doing the fraternity thing" and making his way through school. Considering academics were never a significant challenge, Paul allowed himself to rest a bit on his laurels. Meanwhile, he was becoming very seriously involved with his girlfriend at the time (now his wife) who was going to school in Utah, and decided he wanted to be closer to her. His past experience prevented him from worrying about the hassles of relocation, and the skiing was arguably the best in the country, so Paul and a couple of his friends transferred to Brigham Young University.

Being Catholic at a primarily Mormon school did not turn out to be much of a problem for Paul. Pursuing dual degrees in Finance and Marketing while maintaining a full ski schedule kept him fairly busy. Paul did not work during the course of the school year rather preferring to spend his summers earning money to hold him over. He describes his manual labor jobs as "the most completely un-fun things you could do." But whether he was hauling cement, painting houses, or working the night shift at a grocery store warehouse, Paul gave it a 100% effort. He always remembered what his father had impressed upon him: "There is nothing wrong with doing any kind of work, whether it's digging ditches or anything else." And besides, if he did not have to work while school was in session it left more time for skiing!

Paul graduated mid-semester Magna Cum Laude in the winter of 1982, and still had no clear idea of a future career path. "I didn't feel I learned a lot in college. I had no vision of what I wanted to do. Some people do, I didn't." After taking some time off to be a "ski bum," Paul applied and was accepted to the graduate program at Stanford University hoping things would somehow unfold to his advantage. "I applied to graduate school not at all because I wanted to, but in the early eighties it was *THE* thing to do." There was a six month interim period before his graduate studies were to begin, and he thought it might serve him well to use the time to earn some extra money. Paul's brother-in-law was selling radio advertising at the time in Seattle and had suggested that it might be an option.

"What exactly is it you do?" Paul asked his brother-in-law, and after hearing the outline, thought it sounded "interesting." He would have an opportunity to learn about different businesses, interact with people, and make money, but Paul still was not too sure about the notion of being a salesman. "I never pictured myself selling. I guess I figured I would somehow be sitting in a room making money because someone thought I was a smart guy. I didn't really think I was going to have to do something," Paul adds with a smile. Nonetheless, he entered the six month "Sales Account Executive Training Program" at KIRO AM/FM in Seattle and life as a "salesman" became a reality.

Despite the stigma of being a "salesman," Paul discovered almost immediately that he did in fact really enjoy the whole idea of the radio business. It had a certain sizzle and "show biz" quality that gave the salespeople the illusion that they were involved in a glamorous business. "I probably wouldn't have been so enamored with the idea if I had been selling industrial shelving." In a short period of time, Paul exceeded not only his company's expectations in sales, but his own as well. Perhaps most stimulating for Paul was being able to learn about so many other kinds of businesses. In addition to becoming a generalist, he realized that he was also a decent seller, and it was not so degrading to be known as a salesman. "Business always gets a bad wrap, and salespeople are the lowest common denominator, but I found out it doesn't have to be something negative." After training had concluded, Paul was offered full-time employment with the station. There was good money involved, and at only 22 years of age, that was reason enough to forget about grad school and enter the work force.

In his first year as a salesman, Paul made $36 thousand. "I couldn't believe anyone could make more money than that. My buddies who were engineers and attorneys were grinding away for $20 thousand, and I was having fun making so much more." For the next two years Paul knocked on doors and became what he calls a "sales animal." He knew the more he hustled, the more money he could make, but he tried to keep his new found success in perspective. "No matter what you do, you should never think you have arrived because there is that much more potential out beyond, and you're going to look back and think you can do something way greater than that." Paul still did not look into the future. He never thought it was important to be thinking about and planning his next moves, so when a new job offer arose, it took him by surprise.

Being the number one salesperson at the station was very rewarding for Paul. But when they offered him a lucrative position managing two radio stations in Kansas City, he accepted without hesitation. At 24 years of age, Paul was the youngest major market radio station general manager in the country. To add to the pressure, they also happened to be two of the worst stations in the company. Already full of self-doubt for making a decision to step into something he virtually knew nothing about, Paul realized instantly that he had walked into "a hornet's nest." The challenge was unbelievable, and if anything could go wrong it would. All of a sudden Paul had a title, more than average money and considerable power, but the hardships far outweighed the benefits. He recalls being in his office sometimes "just wanting to cry, but thinking it wasn't becoming for a man in a suit." Paul learned through this experience that "success and failure are absolute impostors because you are given a title and respect, and you're still the same person you were before. It's an interesting reality."

The struggle continued for the next four years, but Paul claims this "baptism of fire" taught him valuable lessons. Plus, he had the distinguished or dubious honor of firing Rush Limbaugh who went on to become one the most successful personalities in the history of radio. Paul felt that in the end the managing aspect was just too much drudgery, and besides, he was much better at selling. It was a tough decision to elect to leave the security and comfort of being a "big fish in a little pond," but Paul needed to make a change. So at 28 years of age when Paul relinquished his position as station manager, he headed back into sales. But this time it was not advertising air time sales, it was the selling of the radio stations themselves. This was big business where it is eat or be eaten in an arena of high ticket items, and only the strong survive. "I knew nothing about the brokerage business, I knew nothing about how it worked." Paul was told by his peers that he was "chasing lightning in a bottle." But he was attracted to that lightning, and the heat it generated.

In 1988, Paul started working in Washington, D.C. with AMERICOM, and almost immediately understood the intensity and genuine drama associated with his new line of work. He started small, selling comparatively modest stations to reasonably diminutive buyers, and used these accomplishments to master the skills necessary to advance into more significant markets. With relative speed, Paul became a notable figure in this exclusive sales society, and eventually wound up in one of the largest radio markets in the country, Dallas, Texas. Making a transition to Star Media Group, Paul had laid the foundation for his success. In 1992, his transactional sales volume exceeded $50 million, in 1993 it was $82 million, in 1994 his figures went beyond $135 million, and in 1995, Paul generated $235 million in sales.

Unlike some salespeople, Paul has no trouble crediting a portion of his success to plain good luck. He thinks that people have a tendency to take personal credit for all the good things and lament the bad, rather than allow fate to play a role. Though Paul believes that one can create his own good luck, he also contends that "a good chunk of your success and a good chunk of your failure, you didn't really deserve." Deserving or not, Paul seems to be comfortably gravitating toward the successful end of the spectrum. He is always aware of his success in that he wants to benefit "from the intensity of the moment" rather then become obsessed with his own accomplishments. "The more you do to feed your own ego, the more it will haunt you. You have to fight to keep your perspective because the same success you're revelling in will strangle you."

"Conducting sales that involve massive quantities of money is completely different than selling anything else at any other level," Paul says. These kinds of transactions shape destinies. When you are "selling at the top of the pyramid," you have to pay close attention to everything. "It's not the best player who wins, it's the guy who plays best." Paul tries to keep in mind that most people want to bend and shape the world into a vision that is most comfortable for them, and make it a place where their own personal perception is a reality. Paul theorizes that you "can bombard people with facts, bombard them with logic, and you can wax eloquent. But until you figure a way in their maze to get to their center, you will not be successful." This has proven to be a pivotal challenge for Paul, and he is constantly searching for new ways to communicate with clients in their own language.

There is no immediate gratification to be realized in these types of sales either. Therefore, patience and the waiting game become integral factors, not to mention having to be very thick-skinned. "It's not brain surgery in terms of complexity, but is brain surgery in terms of the consequences. The highs are so high and the lows are so low. You can work on a deal for six, nine months or a year and watch it evaporate overnight." Paul is unyielding when it comes to honesty because the stakes are so high, and the game so refined, that one simply cannot afford to take the risk. "You are forced to be honest if you want to be a long term player. If you cut corners, you will never survive at the top levels of business. You can make a living, just not at the top."

Regardless of the size of the sale, for Paul the basics remain the same. Whether it is the written law or not, manipulation is to some degree a part of all sales, but it does not have to be a negative factor. Paul has a deep respect and appreciation for the "human element," and reasons that it is very possible to accomplish whatever you need to do while keeping your character intact. "Everyone deserves your attention and everyone deserves to feel important. When someone does not show me a basic level of respect, I get angry. No one deserves to be shown lack of respect, I don't care what they do." People will react to respect and be much more willing to establish some kind of working relationship. People react to nearly any stimulus, and Paul feels it is sometimes more effective to be an "observer than salesman." His ability to read people has led him to subscribe to the belief that "everyone is selling all the time," and further adds, "Until you can understand and react to someone else, you are fighting a battle of motivation with one hand tied behind your back."

Nonetheless, he is driven by competition and never wants anyone to beat him to the punch in a given sales environment. Paul still occasionally battles the stigma of being classified as a salesman, but says the "negative baggage is a small price to pay for the success and for the opportunity."

Regardless of his success and his ability to mastermind million dollar deals everyday, Paul is not a "workaholic." Yes, he works very hard, not constantly, but most times just a little harder than his competitors. Paul would like to tell you it has all been the result of hard work, but truthfully he says, "I've been blessed with fantastic good luck." Paul is an organized thinker, but he would certainly never be asked to speak at a goal-setting convention! He has theories and philosophies that he constantly updates and changes, but has never been the type to make an itemized wish-list of successes. It is the hunt not the kill, and Paul derives most of his pleasure from simply putting together the deal.

Above all else, Paul loves to play, and I would guess his work is merely a means to that end. Another mountain to climb, river to raft, slope to ski, or plane to jump from, and he will be there. The higher the risk, the happier he will be. Paul Leonard plays his high stakes game for keeps, and he usually wins.

To Paul, the secret of success is: "Doing a lot of little things better than my competition, rather than trying to invent a fireball of greatness. Whether it is prospecting, assessing needs, servicing a client, or simply enduring.... most of the battle is won if you just do a little bit better than the next guy. Secondly, and perhaps more importantly, I enjoy everyone. Find a way to find the human race fascinating and you will enjoy life and succeed."

• • • • • • • •

Paul Leonard's personal vision of greatness:

"Great men do great things when nobody is looking. Great people are often those that are not seen, and their greatness is rewarded in ways we don't sometimes see or understand. If a person does great things even though they are seemingly invisible, they will attract others. I wouldn't mind being one of those guys."

Where is Paul now?

Paul is still rocking the radio world. An August 1997 issue of the Wall Street Journal listed his most impressive coup, an acquisition worth $1.2 billion. When I asked him if this was enough for retirement, he laughed and simply said "not yet."

The Introvert

"The ability to concentrate and use your time well is everything if you want to succeed in business or almost anywhere else, for that matter."

Lee Iacocca with William Novak
Iacocca: An Autobiography (1984)

The Introvert

When thinking of the best salesmen in the country, words like dynamic, powerful, and aggressive immediately jump to mind. We envision a perfectly tailored Armani suit, just the right tie, a hint of cologne, and a fancy car with all the bells and whistles. We see slick. We see flash. We see the guy who walks in and takes over. We don't see shy. We don't see quiet. We don't even notice the guy who sits alone at the back of the room nervous about the crowd. So if you're not careful, you might miss Mike Pexa. He's the passive, unobtrusive salesman just doing his thing. And his thing happens to be insurance. Out of more than 13,000 agents at the Farmers Insurance Group, Mike is the best of the best, being named "Agent of the Year" for two consecutive years. His extraordinary underwriting profitability numbers have broken company records, and set new precedents in the industry.

Mike Pexa doesn't consider himself a good salesman, never has, never will. He works hard, does his job well, and hopes the rest falls in place. We should all be so lucky! If you were to look up "nice guy" in the dictionary, you would probably find a picture of Mike—smiling, as always. He is genuine, sincere, and I would be quite surprised if a dishonest thought ever crossed his mind. Mike wages a daily war against the stigma attached to being an "insurance salesman," and resents his profession being regarded as "just a notch above the used car salesman." But if there is anyone that can do it, Mike is surely the one to bring dignity to the cause. He represents all that is good in business, and it's refreshing to see a personification of integrity that illuminates the sometimes cloudy world of sales.

At five years of age, Mike announced he was going to be an insurance man. Not a fireman or a doctor—an insurance man. Mike admits that it has a rather comical ring to it, but swears it is the truth. His father was an agent in Alameda, California, and Mike doesn't recall if it was the paperwork, the files, the briefcase, or his father's enthusiasm, but something seemed intriguing about the insurance business. "My father would get a kick out of it. He would drag me around to company functions and I would recite to everyone what I wanted to be." Mike's father was very pleased with his son's interest in the business, and had him on the phone telemarketing at the age of 12!

Needless to say, Mike's father had a huge impact on his career. His father was a quiet, shy man who was raised in a monastery. Mike says his father had no real conception of money, "he was very idealistic. He believed that you did things for the right reasons." Mike feels he inherited those things from his father, and his voice is filled with admiration and respect when he talks about growing up with such a "good" man. Mike is proud that he was able to follow in his father's footsteps, but the path to insurance sales wasn't as straight and as sure as once envisioned by a precocious five-year-old.

The summer Mike turned sixteen his father came up with this "great idea." Instead of going to summer camp at Yosemite, one of the most beautiful places in the world to be meeting attractive sixteen-year-old girls, Mike could go to the Farmers Insurance Group Agency Career Training Program. To this day he doesn't know how his father talked him into it, but that is where Mike spent what should have been the greatest summer of his life. Mike recalls, "I endured about three weeks in the class and I learned something big. There was no way in the world I was going to become an insurance agent!" He had concluded that these people were "sadistic and nuts." The rejection. The selling. Mike said, "I'm an introvert, I'm quiet, no way," and moved on.

But he didn't have to move far because in the very same training class was a manager from K-Mart. Mike and the K-Mart manager became fast friends, and at sixteen, a job in sporting goods sounded infinitely more interesting than selling insurance. So on June 23rd Mike got his first job. (Coincidentally, it was also on June 23rd that Mike got his driver's license, and in later years, it was on June 23rd that he got his second job, on June 23rd that he got married, and though he tried to get his insurance license on June 23rd, it fell just short on June 18th!) Anyway, the job in sporting goods at K-Mart turned out rather well. Mike was given responsibilities he "didn't think most sixteen-year-olds would get." Within a few months he was handling ordering, and eventually he ran the whole department on his own on Sundays. Mike remembers being "allowed to make decisions, and when I made bad ones, the manager would sit down with me and discuss why." This got him off to a solid start in the work environment, but soon he would have to consider school.

School—what a dilemma for Mike. He doesn't consider himself an extremely academic person. "I got good grades and took all college prep classes, but that doesn't make me academic." By this time Mike had started what he considered to be an even better job with Alpha Beta Food Stores. He knew a lot of people who had gone to college and worked really hard to get a job, but his thought was: "If I already have a great job, why do I need to go to college?" Valid point, but he still felt he should give it a try for his father's sake. So Mike did it all—worked at night and went to school during the day. He started bagging groceries, and was quickly promoted through the ranks to Assistant Manager. At 20 years old Mike was making $36,000 a year and living at home. Inevitably something was going to have to be sacrificed. Mike had always looked at school as a means to an end, but it looked like formal education would soon be taking a back seat.

Mike eventually accumulated about 90 college credits, but never completed enough courses to obtain his degree. "This is still a thorn in his side. My friends all have degrees and are a group of highly intelligent, accomplished people, and I consider myself the flunky of the group. It really bothers me. I regret it, but I haven't closed the book on it yet". For the next 6 1/2 years Mike worked at the grocery store. Though he still had not reconsidered the insurance profession, he was becoming increasingly dissatisfied with his work. "One of the things that always frustrated me about life was that if you worked for someone it didn't matter how hard you tried or how good you were, especially in union affiliation, you didn't make any more than the guy standing next to you." In early 1984, it was apparent that Alpha Beta was going to be leaving the Sacramento area. They offered him a job, but he declined. Mike was getting married and had to make a quick career change. "I figured I was young, and I remembered having a childhood interest in the insurance business, so I gave it a shot."

By February of 1985, Mike was a full-time insurance agent. It was then that he realized he was still an introvert, he was still shy, and he "wasn't going to be much of a salesperson." So rather than give in to his fears, Mike devised what he called his "master plan." The plan was this: If the "average Joe" out there could sit down at a table with 10 people, they could probably get an average of 2 to 3 clients. But Mike figured with his personality, if he approached those same 10 people, he would only get maybe one client. Therefore, he turned it into a numbers game. "What I did was work hard and work smart. I concluded that I needed to see 30 people in the same amount of time it took the "average Joe" to see 10 to do the same job."

Through time and experience the numbers game paid off. Ultimately, Mike began closing not just one in 10, but 3, 4, and 5 out of 10. And he wasn't just seeing 10 people, he began seeing 20 and 30 people, so the numbers kept increasing and increasing. "I think the strategy and attitude I used when I was just getting started is the single biggest thing that helped me in sales." Despite the numbers, Mike has never been able to overcome his shyness. He still doesn't feel he has a particular talent where sales are concerned, but he does have a lot of personal pride; he won't give up. Mike tries to be conscious of his weaknesses and handle them the best he can. Even after ten years, Mike admits that he "hates cold calls," and it is still difficult to phone existing clients or new referrals. "I get nervous all the time, but my fear of failing is much greater and a much bigger driving force than the simple reluctance to call." Lucky for Mike, success has enabled him to hire people to deal with most direct "cold calls," but he will never forget the early "torture of having to dial up a stranger and ask questions about their insurance."

Mike has never tried to "sell," so consequently it was an even bigger challenge to try to "close" a sale. He decided that he would have to make himself into a salesman without being pushy and tough. He would have to develop a style that he could adjust for his kind of personality and rely on his solid strengths to succeed. "I'm a poor salesman, but I'm very organized," Mike says, and that's what worked for him. His associates have gone so far as to call him "Felix Unger" in reference to the neurotically meticulous character from the "Odd Couple." Mike is determined to always have the answers for his clients, and no matter what, follow-up on everything. He believes that organizing even the smallest tasks keeps one in control of a situation. And if the task is too big, "break it down into a small one." Mike credits the ability to organize a strong factor in minimizing his fear of making the sale. He turns it into a methodical process rather than "hard press to get something," and it makes it easier to approach potential clients. He confesses that this strategy may take a bit more time, but it seems to be worth the wait!

Currently servicing 3,200 families in the city of Sacamento, and having written well over 10,000 policies in his career, Mike concludes that the actual numbers have little to do with it now. "It's how many people I can see today without killing myself and taking away from my family." Mike knows he can "afford to be selective." At the beginning, most agents will write policies for the sake of writing policies and hope for the best. But Mike has learned that people's problems generally don't go away, and a bad policy will have trouble turning itself into a good one. The solution is just to take your time and give the clients the attention they need. "If a client takes six hours, it takes six hours. No matter how good a salesman you are, you cannot lose people out the back door or you will be running for the rest of your career."

"Work smarter and harder" has always been a useful credo for Mike. His idea of "working smarter" is to make it easier on yourself as well as the client. And that prospect is twofold: provide better service and run a better business. First, convinced that people do not shop price as much as we might like to believe, the focus needs be on having everything available that the customer needs. "Try to be as universal as you can, make it one-stop shopping." Convenience will get and keep clients. Except for life insurance, which is "sold", all other kinds of insurance (auto, home, etc.) are "bought." Translated: "They are going to have to buy it somewhere, so it might as well be from me." And if Mike provides not only the right service, but a wide selection of services, he increases his possibility of obtaining a client.

Second, sales figures and numbers aside, Mike is adamant about running a good business. He considers himself a businessman before he considers himself an insurance salesman, and this gives him a distinct competitive edge. "Teaching selling skills is obsolete. The new thought pattern should be to teach business skills." From Mike's side of the fence, selling has essentially nothing to do with running the business. He has seen a thousand agents who are better salesmen, but if you "walk into their office, it's a mess. There is no organization." Mike's experiences with being tongue-tied and scared lend credibility to his notion that "people skills can be developed." But if there is no management of paperwork, systems or follow through, there is no business. And without a good business, it won't be long before there is nothing to sell. Mike strongly suggests finding a way to get an "administrative edge," because from his standpoint, it's his business skills that set him apart from the rest. He acknowledges fellow agents who are also top producers, but you walk into their office you have to "gingerly step from the door to a chair to avoid tripping over files." Mike isn't like that, he runs a "tight ship" with a smart crew. "Communicate in the office, and be sure to hire the right people. You're only as good as your employees, and unfortunately you get what you pay for."

Business skills or not, Mike has risen to stardom, and he has done it quickly. Most people in the insurance field do not head there for huge sums of money. Mike says that most of the agents he knows live "very nice, comfortable income lifestyles." They don't do extravagant things, or drive extravagant cars. There may be agents rivalling Mike's income, but it's a safe bet that they have been in the business for 30 years or more. In the 12 years that Mike has been a Farmers' agent, his sales figures have been nothing short of miraculous. Working on a point system of "sales counts," Mike has proven that records were made to be broken. His first year he wrote a sales count of

2,400, by his second year he hit 3,800, his fourth year totalled 7,000, and in 1994 after being named Agent of the Year twice, his annual sales count was at 22,500. The next eligible agent had a sales count of 12,000. Mike has been elected to the President's Council nine times, which is comprised of the top 75 agents in an agent force of 13,000. In laymen's terms, he has accomplished levels of success selling insurance that few have ever attained.

Men like Mike do not seem to actually fit in the world of sales. He concedes that he wasn't made for this kind of work. Math, calculus, and computers are his love. He laughs when he tells me, "I'm the type who could get lost in the Internet for a week, come out unshaven, and never even miss the outside world." This is the kind of man who would be content doing facts and figures all day and never talk to a soul. Nonetheless, fate smiled and Mike ended up where he is. "I've got the greatest job in the world today," he confesses. "I get paid to take care of people and make friends. That's how I earn my living. It's incredible."

But do not be fooled, there is plenty of hard work involved too! Mike and his family are no strangers to the concept. He considers Lee Iaccoca and his grandfather to be his mentors. Lee Iaccoca gets the nod because he's such a "savvy" businessman, and Mike envies that kind of thinking. Not to mention he drives one of Iaccoca's Dodge Vipers! His grandfather, on the other hand, earns Mike's respect through pure guts. Mike tells me the story of how his great-grandfather was killed in a mining accident when his grandfather was only in the sixth grade. Mike's grandfather dropped out of school and went to work to help raise the family. He worked in mines and oil refineries his entire life, and at night would work on building a house. Mike remembers when he graduated from eighth grade his grandfather wrote him a note, and Mike suddenly realized that this man was basically illiterate. "I was just shocked, horrified. But as fast as I was horrified, I was proud of the fact the he worked so hard. He did everything. Here's a man who built his own house. I always admired how hard he worked." Mike still keeps the timely note his grandfather gave him to remind him of the real meaning of "hard work."

Mike continues to work diligently. He is constantly redefining his goals and looking for ways to better himself and his agency in the future. He toys with the idea of going back to school. "I'll finish, I really will, but I'm at a point right now where I don't think education stops with school. If I were to back up today to attend a university to learn about geometry or calculus or whatever I need to graduate, that wouldn't benefit my clients and my business today." Mike would like to think he's learning something new every day, and hopefully applying it positively to his business and his clients. So for now, he will focus on the job at hand and worry about the diploma later.

Outside of work, Mike is a family man. No surprise there. He has a wife and two beautiful children (and another on the way!). Mike wants to set an example and teach his children the value of work. "I don't care how smart you are, if you don't combine it with hard work, you're not going to get ahead in this world." He doesn't consider himself a person who goes to motivational clinics and sales classes all day.

Mike's sole source of inspiration and motivation is his own family.

Talking to Mike Pexa proves that there are no stereotypes when it comes to success. Maybe part of his secret is the fact that you simply cannot help but like him. Hard work, smart work, any way you look at it, this nice guy didn't finish last.

To Mike, the secret of success is: "Being able to go into the sales setting and you do not have to make the sale—you're only there to do a great job for your client. When you get to this point in your life and you're truly able to do the right things for right reasons then you have made it."

• • • • • • • •

Mike Pexa's personal vision of greatness:

"I want to redefine the standards of insurance. My career is just starting. If I were a doctor, I'd still be in my internship. I don't see myself retiring - in my business you don't have to. There are guys who are 85-90 years of age who are still insurance agents. I see myself being that way. I want to take it to a new level. I want to feel like I've set new sights and new standards. I'd like people in my business to say, "he redefined the professionalism of an insurance agent." I think that my industry needs a lot of work in that area, and I'd like to think I contributed to that."

Where is Mike now?

Mike continues to be among the very best at Farmers. Again he was named to Presidents Council which recognizes top agents, and has begun to expand and change his focus within the company. In 1997 Mike started teaching agents from across the country how to run their business, and feels that he has truly found his niche, and that this avenue will be his most rewarding success.

The All-American Girl

"Far and away the best prize that life offers is the chance to work hard at work worth doing."

Theodore Roosevelt
Labor Day Address, Syracuse NY (1903)

The All-American Girl

Driving through the fog after dark in the sleepy town of Scarborough, Maine isn't exactly where you would think to be looking for one of the nation's most successful saleswomen. But she is here somewhere. She seemed very sure about the directions over the phone and even confirmed with a fax. The house must be nearby. She told me not to eat first so that we could go out for lobster. Finally, tired and hungry, I locate the house numbers and knock on the door. Standing before me is everyone's girl next door, the cheerleader, a petite blonde with enough energy to light up a city block. Karen Vachon is sugar and spice and everything nice, and reached a pinnacle in her sales career of $25 million a year as a heavy-hitting confection salesperson for the American Chicle division of Warner-Lambert.

Once a year, *Selling Magazine* dedicates an issue to all-stars in the field of selling. In 1995, Karen was among those listed and her story stood out as rather unique. People don't generally give much thought to the world of selling gum, candy and packaged goods, but it is indeed a very competitive and substantial business. If you do not want to get lost in the shuffle, you had best have something special up your sleeve to truly prosper within the confines of corporate America. Karen's evolution isn't necessarily rags to riches, but instead is representative of an honest look at what it takes to work from the bottom to the top. It's fitting that Karen sold sweets, because it would be difficult to meet a more sincere, friendly person. But don't think that makes her a pushover; to the contrary, Karen Vachon is a real powerhouse.

It is hard to believe that so much can be put into such a small package, but when Karen ordered each of us two lobsters, french fries, steamers and a couple of beers, I knew she meant business! Very relaxed and comfortable in a one-on-one situation with a stranger, it is easy to see how sales might be the right career choice for her. She admits that it is difficult for her to make an impact on people because of the whole "blonde image," but her accomplishments prove it hasn't been too big of a stumbling block. She takes everything she says very seriously. Karen is an "old school" thinker in that she has an unyielding sense of right and wrong.

Karen Vachon grew up in the affluent bedroom community of Wayland, Massachusetts. She always thought of herself as the poor kid in a rich neighborhood, and was never overly impressed by the things that money could buy. Her parents were (and still are) in the garden business. Karen watched her family's company grow from a roadside stand to a full-fledged garden center with sixteen greenhouses. At a young age her father and mother instilled in her a solid work ethic and entrepreneurial spirit, but it would be a long time before Karen was focused on a career. She worked on and off throughout high school at the garden center planting seedlings, making flower arrangements, and running the cash register. At the time, she had no clear idea of what she really wanted to do. Her father made her a promise, the same one he had made to her sisters: there would always be a job waiting for her at home, but she would have to experience working for someone else first.

Karen has worked for a lot of someone elses! She seems too young for her years, but once you start sifting through her long list of prior jobs, the mileage element becomes apparent. There is little doubt that Karen was always willing to roll up her sleeves and give it her best shot. Her history proves itself again and again. There is simply no substitute for hard work and a positive attitude. Even when Karen was in Campfire Girls she was pushing herself to be better. Her campfire tribe name was "Tawanka" which means "willing to try." By the time she reached college, Karen was working a total of 40 hours a week at three separate jobs, and at the same time, managing to maintain a 3.5 grade point average. Her early experience consisted primarily of waitressing and housekeeping, so upon completing her Bachelor's degree in Business Administration from New England College, she decided upon a career in restaurant management.

Like many career paths, Karen's took a couple of twists and turns. And nothing can disrupt a straight course from point A to point B quicker than true love. While in college, Karen met someone who she thought was the man of her dreams. He was pursuing a career in broadcasting so Karen decided to table her ambitions and follow him to Seal Harbor, Maine. After all, they were engaged to be married, and Karen being a woman of traditional values, put her career second to her upcoming marriage. But it wasn't quite as simple as passing time while planning a wedding, and Karen's financial situation dictated that she must work. Thinking it would keep her somewhat associated with the restaurant business, she took a job as head baker and cook at the Happy Crab Restaurant in Southwest Harbor, Maine. The restaurant catered to fishermen, meaning that Karen was out of bed at 3:30 A.M., in the car for a 20-minute commute, and ready to bake muffins and flip eggs for $5.00 an hour at the crack of dawn. Karen laughs when she remembers and adds, "it sounded like a good idea at the time."

Things generally rolled along as planned, and Karen's wedding day drew nearer and nearer. Unfortunately, her fiancé had a different outlook on their future. Seems his cold feet couldn't be warmed and the wedding was called off. Karen was devastated. The combination of no money in the bank, and a job that wouldn't pay the rent was forcing some major life changes. Things were looking fairly bleak, so Karen decided to move in with her sister and brother-in-law in Portland, Maine until she could get her feet on the ground. It wasn't long before she gathered what was left of her self-esteem and retreated to the grind of a $5.00 an hour waitressing job. She knew it had to get better than this.

Always trying to keep smiling, Karen looked towards the future. By now she was not only waitressing, but cooking as well. Nothing seemed to be falling into place. She needed something to change, some sort of impetus with which to move on. Always, if we look hard enough, inspiration may be much closer than we think. For Karen it was sitting at one of her tables. A regular customer, a field salesman for Helluva Good Cheese, looked at her and said, "What the hell are you doing at the grill? You should be in sales. You like people, you're outgoing, you like to talk to your customers, you're in the wrong line of work." It was as simple as a suggestion. The wheels began to turn, Karen realized what a good idea it was, and sales certainly meant more money. To Karen, money was an unknown concept, so the thought of having it was more than appealing. Selling just might be the answer.

It didn't take long for Karen to find a part-time entry level sales position. She was a sub-rep for a manufacturer's representative for "something like 60 lines" of giftware. Being the sub-rep meant that she got a small cut of commissions from the direct representatives, and the payments were usually very slow in coming. Nonetheless, she quickly discovered her natural ability to sell. It was exhilarating and challenging. For nine months she worked as hard as she could trying to absorb as much sales experience as possible. The money was only fair at best, and the payments sporadic. Though she was convinced sales was her future, she knew she would have to make a change to something more secure and rewarding.

In July of 1985, Karen was going through her daily ritual of scanning the paper for possible sales positions when she came across an ad for American Chicle. She wasn't sure who American Chicle was, but there were pictures of Dentyne, Trident, Certs, and a number of other brands that were familiar to her. She knew these names, had grown up with them, and immediately thought it might be fun to sell them. She applied and got the job. Karen remembers the interview went very well, but she was told the possibilities for any kind of advancement were nonexistent. The company was very clear in telling her this was not considered an entry level career position, this was considered a part-time job stocking and changing gum displays. She openly told them she wanted to be in sales, would prove herself and they would see it differently. She was sure that somewhere down the line this would become full-time work, and possibly lead to a career.

Karen diligently stocked gum and candy displays at grocery stores and retail outlets throughout the area. And though American Chicle didn't view her job as anything special, Karen took it to heart as a pathway to a serious career. American Chicle is a division of Warner-Lambert, a huge pharmaceutical company focusing on their customers' health and well-being. Karen had done her research and knew that 90% of the population consumes confectionery products, and this company had a comfortable share of the market. She knew a permanent position with this company could lead to bigger things, so she dug in her heels and went to work. A year and two months later it all paid off. American Chicle was taken by storm. Everything Karen Vachon touched turned to gold. First, she was made a full-time representative in southern Maine. From there she became District Sales Manager for the state of Maine with an account volume of $5 million, and finally Regional Account Manager for the northeast with territorial volumes reaching $25 million.

Although very modest when asked about her accomplishments, Karen beams with pride when she begins to detail the results of her labor. In 1993, Karen was the Region Account Manager President's Club Award winner for top sales in her region, and in 1994 she was chosen for a 14-member team of executives and salespeople to re-engineer American Chicle. From an origin of stocking shelves to giving speeches in the boardroom, Karen has earned every bit of the respect she commands. Her co-workers describe her as hard working, honest, emotional, a risk taker, and someone who speaks her mind and doesn't hesitate to challenge the status quo. In her enthusiasm, she gets herself wound up easily and you can readily see her level of excitement elevate when she has a new idea in the works. Some of her colleagues call her "wild thing" because they receive voice mail messages at 4:00 A.M. with her latest brainstorm on how to sell a new program or further build the business.

Personally, Karen believes that her greatest strength is her candor. "Let's face it," she says, "the truth often hurts, but it always feels better once everything is out in the open." She concludes that her customers are more open with her if she is up front with them. She is very proud of the relationships she has built, and is happy that many of her customers are now good friends. To Karen the customer always comes first—no matter what. She has a great deal of trouble with the politics that inevitably creep into the corporate structure, but tries to keep it balanced so that the customer does not suffer. "The key is to listen," Karen tells me. "Listening skills are one of a salesperson's greatest tools, and if they learn how to use them, they will be amazed at the results."

Too often Karen thinks that salespeople fall into a mold of corporate policy that has them saying to their customers, "I can't do that." Karen has "monumental" problems with "I can't." She says she will literally cringe when she hears people say that. Karen is in constant search of the win-win situation, where both the customer and her company benefit. The confectionery products she sold have what is called expandable consumption. This means that the more exposure people have to products, the more likely they will be to consume them. The purchase of a confection product is an 87% impulse purchase, therefore the sell must not only be strong, but creative as well. By limiting themselves to "I can't," Karen believes that salespeople are limiting the scope of their creativity and effectiveness to generate the right sales strategy.

Conviction is an ever-present part of Karen's success. If something should be different, she'll go out and make the changes. In the early stages of her career the dollar signs dangled like carrots in front of her, and growing financial possibilities dictated some of the changes she was making. Over time, she discovered that the money was "considerably over-rated." She was making an extremely prosperous living, but the time demands were so strenuous that it didn't seem worth it to her in the long run. Karen began to make changes in her goals when she realized the destructive nature of using money as a "measurement of success." The overall nature of the process made her take a long, hard look at herself and realize that it really wasn't about the money, it was about personal gratification for a job well done. She is sincere when she says, "I don't need the quick promotion. I want to enjoy my job every inch of the way. You don't have to advance me quickly through my career. Give me the experience and let me work hard—the money will come. I believe that."

Customer service is the key to everything for Karen. To her the growth of business revolves around taking care of the customer. She tries to look at business through the eyes of the customer while thinking in general terms of how to react as a consumer. Going into stores to watch how the shoppers make decisions was always helpful in creating new and better displays. Karen refused to be the average salesperson that merely picks up an order for product and moves on. She wants to make a difference, and be the salesperson of choice rather than necessity. "The key is relationships. Thinking in terms of people working with people, instead of salesman working with business, has made the difference."

When Karen isn't out on sales calls, she can be found in the basement office of her three story Scarborough home. Now married, and with two young boys, Karen has found that being a working mother has proven to be a tremendous challenge. She has found it difficult to give 100% of herself in both directions, yet continues to try. "It's always a struggle." Her workspace is a wondrous combination of toys, desks, phones and paper. She considers herself "administratively disorganized," and it does appear as though a small bomb may have gone off causing destruction and disarray. She is quick to remind me that she does in fact have a good memory and is very organized in her mind. Observing her daytimer coming apart at the seams, and with a sprawling calendar, it certainly must be so! The phone never stops ringing, and the follow-up seems endless. Karen tries not to get too bogged down with organizational aspects, but rather stay focused on systematically tackling the immediate problem at hand. She places a great deal of importance on delegating work whenever necessary, and believes salespeople could accomplish more if they didn't try to keep an eye on every aspect of their work themselves.

"Either you have it or you don't." That's how Karen feels when asked about the sales effort in general. She has a strong opinion about the fact that sales people are born, not made. She prefers to think of success in sales as instinctive, and doesn't feel it has all that much to do with being smart. And if you do have "the gift" to sell, you can never give up. Karen is driven by a fear of failure. That's why she works the long hours and makes the sacrifices. "It's okay to be motivated by that fear. After all, motivation is motivation." Karen has a tendency to think that most people become so absorbed in their work that they lose sight of everything else. "Success to me is being able to balance my family life and my career," Karen says, but it is seldom that easy. "Sometimes it is a huge struggle not to get caught up in the frustration of being pulled a thousand different directions at once." You wouldn't think this golden girl had anything hiding behind her smile, but she admits that she does have quite a temper. When things go awry, she is definitely not the type to shout explosively or make an unruly scene. She simply cries. "It's not a weakness, sometimes you just have to have a breakdown or two!"

Dale Carnegie's book, *How To Win Friends and Influence People,* has made a significant impact on Karen's life. She took her first Dale Carnegie course when she was working as a waitress, and swears that "simply everyone should read this book or attend the seminar." Through the Carnegie teachings she discovered the benefits of being genuinely nice to other people, as well as remaining constantly enthusiastic with a positive attitude. People respond to her inherent kindness, she gives people praise when they deserve it, and she knows how greatly it has helped her own career. Always the cheerleader for the underdog, Karen never loses sight of the light at the end of the tunnel—no matter how dark it may seem. She urges those she is close to "operate by gut decision, trust their inner sense, and move on the course that feels the most right."

Every salesperson has their own definition of success. Karen's has always been to "have quality of life rich with diversity and experience, all mixed together with a finely tuned balance between family and job." Her definition has remained the same throughout her career, yet the reality at the moment is that her balance may be off center, and leaning too far towards her work. She has recently made a decision to take a career sabbatical and follow her husband's calling to Switzerland for two years. Karen's new focus will be on her family, learning a new culture, mastering two languages, and improving her computer skills. When she returns to sales, she feels she will be armed with a more "worldly approach," which will ultimately create even more success for the All-American girl.

To Karen, the secret of success is: "Four things: Know what you're good at (and do it), genuinely care about people, listen and follow through."

• • • • • • • •

Karen Vachon's personal vision of greatness:

"To be a good person and set examples. Money is small. I want to be rich, not with money, but with experience. Money is only to get by—to have the basics. I want to enrich the lives of people around me."

Where is Karen now?

Karen has returned from Switzerland and has resettled in her home in Scarborough, Maine. After a hiatus from the working world she has decided to test her sales skills in some very uncharted waters. Karen has accepted a position at a company called Alprofil in Westbrook, Maine where she hopes to put some of her Warner-Lambert skills to work. Alprofil is an aluminum extrusion company that sells bulk extrusion, hardware and components, as well as customized solutions for modular work stations, benches, tables, machine guarding and other custom applications. She loves the challenge of her new work and she tells me that in the end "sales is sales, and if you can sell and you have product knowledge, you can sell anything!"

THE TEACHER

"A teacher affects eternity; he can never tell where his influence stops."

Henry Adams
The Education of Henry Adams (1907)

The Teacher

Webster's Dictionary defines "teach" as "To communicate knowledge or skill. To provide instruction in. To give insight by example or experience." The ability to teach is a true gift. We all remember our best teachers, and hold them dear in our hearts. We remember them because they genuinely cared for us, and wanted us to reach our highest goals and maximize our greatest potential. Scott Magnesen is one of those very special teachers. Quietly, conservatively, and without fanfare, he makes a daily impact on the lives of over 4,000 people. They are his clients, as well as his students. He gives them lessons about the future based upon his steady success in the past. He believes in their dreams and helps them reach for the stars. He arms them with knowledge to make the important decisions in life. He instructs them. And just for good measure, he makes them money in the process. But do not become mired in semantics, because whether you call him teacher, financial consultant, or just plain stockbroker, Scott Magnesen is the best in the business. As a Senior Vice President at Dean Witter Reynolds, Inc., this multimillion dollar sales producer believes that educating his own clients and potential clients is the key to success.

Sitting behind a huge mahogany desk, Scott appears awfully young to be in such impressive surroundings. Everything in the office seems enlarged, everything makes a statement. Scott on the other hand appears very nonchalant and conservative, looking as if he might be equally comfortable in a recliner watching a football game. The suit and tie make him look the broker part, but his boundless energy tells you he'd be a success in whatever line of work he may choose. He has a natural ability to put people at their ease, and makes the $1000 investor feel as important as the million dollar heavy-hitter. Regardless, sitting in a room with someone who has capital responsibility for more than several hundred-million dollars worth of investments can be a bit intimidating.

For those of us who have hardly been able to save enough for a down payment on a car, let alone start an investment portfolio, the life of a stockbroker is rather fascinating. For some reason I always believed brokers to be mathematician types with a long list of business degrees, the type of people who have focused their entire college career and post graduate effort on the ins and outs of money matters. But much to my surprise, this broker plays to the beat of a different drum.

Illinois has always been home for Scott Magnesen. He spent his childhood in a closely knit family living in Elmhurst. His father was a school teacher and college administrator, his mother a housewife. Scott has nothing but praise for his parents and how he was raised. He was taught the value of discipline and the power of positive thinking at a young age, and has held onto those constants throughout his life. Scott admits he was "never the smartest, never the best, and never the most popular" growing up, but people have always gravitated toward him. Perhaps it was his underlying energy and charisma, or perhaps it was his gift for music.

Music was Scott's life. He practiced and worked, worked and practiced; music meant discipline, and discipline meant commitment. Scott was quite sure that his future would be the result of his efforts. Percussion was the instrument of choice, and drums his specialty. So when Scott began his curriculum at Northwestern University in Evanston, Illinois, his major was, of course, music. All roads were leading toward a career not only as a performer, but a teacher as well.

While completing his studies at Northwestern, Scott joined the musician's union. He supported himself by playing the drums professionally with a local band. The gigs were bar mitzvahs, weddings, Christmas parties, anything that would give Scott a chance to perform and make a couple of dollars for his efforts. He loved to be in front of a crowd. He loved the rush of adrenaline that you never quite get used to, and he loved the applause. When big-name acts like Carol Lawrence and Maynard Ferguson came to town, he and his fellow musicians were lucky enough to sit in and do some backup work. He had found his comfort zone in front of an audience, and knew it was a place he wanted to stay.

In addition to his unwavering love for and commitment to performing, Scott also had a keen interest in business. Education had always been a focal point in his family, and it seemed natural to want to pursue some sort of postgraduate endeavor. After completing his studies with a Bachelor of Arts degree in Music, Scott thought it might be lucrative to take a closer look at his business interests and try for his M.B.A. (Master of Business Administration). He could continue the musical interests while creating a safety net for himself in case the public performing aspects failed to materialize as he had hoped. He applied to Kellogg Business School at Northwestern University and was accepted. However, since he had no practical experience in the business world, he was required to work for one full year before starting the program.

Scott correctly surmised that something in sales would serve as an adequate prerequisite for any job. Scott is a gifted communicator, and obviously comfortable in the presence of large groups of people. So why not sell something? Maybe jewelry? There was an assistant manager position available at a local jewelry store, and it appeared as good a place as any to start. Scott quickly realized two things: First, retailing is tedious work, and second, he was exceptional at selling. As a manager, he was not necessarily supposed to be concentrating on the actual sale, but nevertheless found himself relaxed with the customers and his sales figures were higher than most of the other staff! Retail certainly was not going to hold Scott's interest for the long haul, but the experience would be enough to establish the proper background for his advanced studies in the world of business.

In addition to his work at the jewelry store, Scott maintained his interest in music, and even managed to find time to mow the lawn for his neighbor, Jim Gee. Jim Gee was born and raised in Hong Kong. His family came to the United States when Jim was in high school, and he taught himself to speak English in order to complete his education. Despite the language barrier, Jim obtained a degree in engineering and later became a very successful stockbroker for Dean Witter Reynolds. He was friendly with the Magnesen family, and had watched Scott grow up. Jim recognized Scott's innate ability to communicate and had a strong hunch that he had the qualifications to be a good broker. Jim told Scott, if he were to commit two years of his life to really making a go of it in the brokerage business, the $13,000 a year salary he was earning at the jewelry store would be long forgotten.

At 22 years of age the thought of anything resembling a salary over $25,000 a year was very appealing. So, Scott took Jim Gee's suggestion to heart and agreed to try being a stockbroker before going back to school. When basic broker training class began, Scott realized what a gamble Jim Gee had taken by hiring him. As each of the new brokers introduced themselves, their names were followed by a list of impressive schools, impressive accomplishments, and impressive experience. When Scott spoke, and his credentials consisted of being a music major with some basic retail knowledge, there might have been a chuckle or two in the room. But he was the "energy kid," and by the end of the month Scott too was impressive—voted "most likely to succeed."

And succeed he did. Needless to say, Scott never went back to school to get his MBA. He did however complete the Senior Account Executive Advanced Training program through Dean Witter's exclusive alliance with the Wharton Business School of the University of Pennsylvania. Scott's gross commissions exceeded six figures in his very first year, and nearly doubled in each of the next two. In his fifth year, at age 28, with $1 million in gross commissions, Scott was named to Dean Witter's Chairman's Club. This honor is given to the top 150 brokers who maintain the highest quality practice for a minimum of three consecutive years. These kinds of accomplishments are almost unheard of for such a young broker. Scott is strictly a retail broker, meaning all his accounts are "ma and pa clients," no company money and no pension fund money. At Dean Witter, Scott personifies success.

Scott is fascinated by his work. He describes it as the "perfect job." Virtually everything in the world affects financial markets, and in turn affects himself and his clients. "No two days are ever the same, and the investment landscape is changing all the time." Scott is a steady and grounded thinker in the face of these constant changes, and his goal is to always, without exception, put his clients' interests first. His role is that of a coach / teacher, not a fortune teller. "No one can read the future," Scott assures, "analysts can't, brokers can't. Reading will only show you what you should have known a year ago." Scott feels that his job as coach / teacher is to provide what he calls "education 101" on the basics, because "the more you understand, the better you will do."

Being an outstanding broker requires integrity at a very deep level. Anyone can take a course to become a stockbroker, but "managing someone's long-term financial future requires a strong commitment." To Scott, a broker has to have enough confidence to build his own business slowly and "forge lasting relationships that will lead to success over time." Scott believes truly successful brokers have to be genuinely concerned about the client's long term needs, be willing to look down the road 20 or 30 years, and be able to make a good decision. "Regardless of what you have the potential to make, you have got to do it right."

As cliché as it may sound, Scott warns brokers not to "let money be your motivator." When his business first began to take off, he is the first to admit that he got caught up in the entire "power trip" that goes with making money. The smart brokers learn quickly not to adjust their lifestyle to their newly found wealth because things are pretty tough the first five years in the brokerage business. "If you adjust your standard of living the moment you have a good month, it could get a bit tight when you have a bad month or two." Again, the key is patience and confidence. Eventually, it will all pay off.

On occasion, Scott has been accused of being too conservative. But he stands by his goal to "get the highest return with the least risk." He chuckles when asked about high risk investments, and tells me I might have an equal chance of profit if I were to take my money to Las Vegas! "Anyone who tries to make money fast will ultimately lose it. There is no fast, easy money." Scott's job is to advise his clients about what they "should" have. When it comes to stocks he's not trading regularly, he won't bend easily. If he strongly thinks a client should not buy something, he will do his best to dissuade them. If they insist, he will either let them buy it somewhere else thereby giving the client full responsibility, or he will tell the client when to buy and sell without much counseling in between transactions.

Scott contends that he can't manage anyone else's money differently than he manages his own. All of Scott's clients are invested in basically the same things, so in essence he only has to watch one portfolio. The investments themselves are chosen according to a client's age, means and needs, but other than that, the stocks and funds are mostly the same. Scott makes it his policy to recommend only those high-quality investments he would consider for himself. Working from this universe, he customizes a portfolio for each client, its contents varying depending upon the factors mentioned before: investor's age, needs, objectives, and investment preferences. Essentially, Scott monitors one very large, cohesive portfolio, and builds individual portfolios from that stable as is appropriate for each client.

The idea is to not just invest money, but to explain the various changes and moves to the client. "Let them be a part of their investment and make sure they know how it all works." Educate, educate, educate—that's it. That's the big secret. Since Scott has always been the champion of the small investor, he has been able to make a huge impact on the people he has taught. From the beginning of his career, Scott has taken the educational approach to marketing. He began speaking at service clubs, community organizations, and public libraries, anywhere he could to promote knowledge and in turn acquire new clients. The whole stock market and investment arena can be a very intimidating place for most people. It is of such foreign soil that we never think to try to understand it. Scott gives people knowledge, that knowledge empowers them, and when they know it, they do not fear it, and hence want to be a part of it—an amazingly simple equation.

One of Scott's strongest philosophies is that the "small investors need loving too!" In fact, that is the name of one of his most successful seminars. Many brokers tend to ignore the "little guys," so Scott structures many of his seminars around basic investing. Most people will learn more in a two hour class with Scott than they will in a month of trying to decipher financial publications. The students in attendance range from couples looking toward retirement to business people who are trying to decide how and where to invest their money. Scott is a powerful, dynamic speaker with a clear and understandable presentation. He credits his past experience in music performance for his ability to be at ease in front of a group. Scott is sure that "performing skills are essential for a broker to have, "and adds that "as a broker you're on stage every minute you're on the phone - you're really on stage the whole day." He is patient with questions, and takes time to "read" the audience and get a feel for who they are and what they need. "How you respond to them has a lot to do with your ultimate success in communicating with them." By being frank and offering knowledgeable insight into the many investment experiences he has had, he has a way of making the people feel very comfortable. By the time the seminar is over, you can't imagine trusting your money to anyone else but Scott!

For those just beginning to invest, Scott's teachings give a sense of hope and excitement that money will be made for the future. He almost prefers the beginners, because "when someone has already made it, it's not as much fun." The biggest reward for Scott is to make a real difference in people's lives. He loves to see the end result, and to hear someone say "I couldn't do it without you." And Scott couldn't do it without a strong positive mental attitude. To achieve a rewarding end result, a successful career has to go through stages. Scott asserts that motivation starts for most as a "fear of failure," followed by a desire for money. If they can get beyond a purely monetary drive, the next stage is to reach motivation through recognition. Scott says "for many recognition is enough, for a few it becomes power." Finally, if everything stays on track, you reach what Scott calls the "richest of all phases of success." This is where the motivation is to "give back to your industry and help others achieve what you have."

Scott's conception is that "success in sales evolves as an individual goes through a learning period and masters their ability to communicate." To him, communication skills may come naturally, but they can be developed and must be developed in order to succeed. He also feels that strength, character and charisma are inherited, but discipline and self-motivation can be learned. "Discipline breeds tenacity, and if you combine that with good communication skills, you'll have someone who can be a huge success." Scott knows there are plenty of "slick" salespeople in the business world, but argues that it's the guy that puts his nose to the grindstone that will win in the long run. "I'll take the grinder over the slick one everyday." To grind through a sales career you have to "have the internal drive to do the same thing over and over, a million times."

And a million more times, Scott will sell his educational philosophies, and millions of dollars more will be invested. Scott personally defines success as the ability to "be the best you can be at a job you like, and be recognized by your peers as a role model." He revises his goals daily, weekly, monthly and annually to make sure he never takes his past accomplishments for granted. But none of those goals are related to personal gain, all are centered on adding new customers, managing more money, better servicing of existing clients, and building his reputation in the investment community. "Goals keep me motivated to work harder," Scott says. And the goals must be working because there is no sign of things slowing down!

But even a broker of this magnitude finds time to put work on the back burner. Scott says his life is "work, family and golf," but tells me his family comes first. He is not really sure about the order of the other two! Scott makes it a point to play golf twice a week, and attacks his game with the same discipline and perseverance he uses at work. He likes the challenge of getting better and has made a solid effort to become an above-average recreational player. At this rate, the Professional Golfer's Association better keep their eyes open! But it's not only golf, Scott is an avid runner and a big fan of most sports.

Music is still a very big part of Scott's life. He can be found entertaining every so often at a company function, but prefers to maintain it at home. Music is "simply an emotional release" for him these days, and finds it relaxing to come home and play the piano after work. Still a member of the local musician's union, Scott has even been known to get a call or two when someone needs a drummer. "Someday I'll perform again when I slow down," he says. "I'll buy my way back in—I'll hire a big band and go on tour."

Time commitments have certainly increased as his success has grown. He manages his time better, and has dedicated weekends to his family. His wife and four sons are his top priority, and hopes that one or more of them will eventually follow in his footsteps in the brokerage business. If they do, they have some rather big shoes to fill.

To Scott, the secret of success is: "Enjoying what you are doing, believing in yourself, maintaining a positive attitude and a consistent work discipline while having fun along the way."

• • • • • • • •

Scott Magnesen's personal vision of greatness:

"To be a person with positive self-esteem and self-image built by good works throughout life. To reach the highest level of skills in my respective profession and help others develop that same skill."

Where is Scott now?

Scott is still at Dean Witter and continues to build his client base and escalate sales figures.

The Die Hard

"The person who makes a success of living is the one who sees his goal steadily and aims for it unswervingly. That is dedication."

Cecil B. DeMille
Sunshine and Shadow (1955)

The Die Hard

Transitions and successions are a natural part life. They are also a part of most jobs and professions. Students become teachers, secretaries become managers, officers become generals, actors become movie stars, dental hygienists become millionaires and interns become surgeons. Wait a minute—dental hygienist to millionaire? Not exactly within the realm of natural progression, and most would have to conclude that it must be the lottery. Leslie Stanford agrees it has something to do with luck, but it all depends on how you look at it. A millionaire at the age of 27, Leslie now has an income that exceeds $100,000 per month. This multilevel marketing mogul for Herbalife International is living proof that "if there's a will, there's a way."

When talking with friends, multilevel marketing may not be the first topic that comes to mind. But Leslie is one friend who might have something fairly substantial to say about it. Multilevel marketing is not the type of profession a person generally grows up aspiring to, but that's changing. In fact, the entire perception of the industry is more favorable than ever, and multilevel marketing is now receiving positive reviews from many influential members of the business community. And to further substantiate its acceptance, there are now courses offered at universities and colleges teaching its marketing concepts.

There are no prerequisites for multilevel marketing in the working world. It just seems to be one of those opportunities that presents itself along the way by happenstance. This kind of selling does not require any special skills or former experience because its only criteria is desire and determination. The draw being that it is a business opportunity that is wholly available to anyone who wants to get involved.

In spite of some skeptics, companies like Herbalife International (with worldwide sales in 1996 of more than a billion dollars) have turned their unique marketing style into a virtual gold mine. Those who have had the incentive to take it seriously enough to commit the time and energy necessary to call it a career have reaped rewards beyond their wildest dreams. Herbalife International sells weight management products, food and dietary supplements, and personal care products. They sell their products through a network of approximately one million distributors worldwide. In a marketing system such as this, new distributors pay for a what is know as an "international distributor pack" and receive a discount on Herbalife products. As a distributor the idea is to retail products, recruit new distributors, and teach them to do the same while they advance through the system. As they move up, distributors increase their product discounts and earn royalties on their recruits' sales thereby creating an ever-growing flow of residual income. It is an incredibly simple concept, and perhaps that is what drives the vehicles of doubt in the minds of so many. Some say the dollar figures are so enormous that it is just too good to be true. Maybe so, but a die hard like Leslie will tell you "nothing is too good to be true anymore."

Growing up in Calgary, Alberta in Canada, Leslie had what she considers a very "normal" childhood. Her father was in real estate, and her mother a housewife. Before the age of computers, new real estate listings were printed on what were known as "green sheets." Leslie remembers being a little girl and helping her father update these "green sheets." She was his "cheerleader," and loved to see her father sell a house. Leslie observed that the harder her father worked, the more money he made. (Later in life this concept would have a certain symmetry to it because the very same principle is the driving force behind the success in her career.) Leslie grew up and eventually attended college at the University of Alberta in Edmonton. She decided to pursue studies in a secure field with plenty of job opportunities, and seeing as her family dentist had told her it was a "wonderful career for a girl," Leslie set her sights on becoming a hygienist. Never envisioning herself in "the business world in a power suit behind a desk," she secretly lived the fantasy of graduating from college and "marrying the perfect guy and having a storybook life."

"Cleaning teeth and educating people about oral hygiene is a laugh a minute, let me tell you," Leslie recalls with a grin. But it was steady income, it was in fact a job, and she hadn't looked too much further down the road than that. Then, as if by magic, Leslie met her knight in shining armor, and her life began spiraling in a completely different direction. Her fiancé was an attorney in Los Angeles, and she quickly made arrangements for a move to California and prepare for a wedding. The fantasy was becoming a reality. Leslie wasted little time getting settled. She leased a condo on the beach in Marina Del Rey, leased furniture, leased a car—leased, leased, leased. They were going to be married soon, so finances were of little concern. Well, unfortunately (but fortunately in the long run!), Leslie's fairytale came to an abrupt end. Seems her knight's shining armor was a bit tarnished, and he had been supplementing his income in some rather unscrupulous ways. So the wedding was off, the relationship was over, and as quickly as you can say "the check's in the mail," Leslie found herself in a house full of furniture without a hope in the world of paying for any of it.

After adding up all of her bills and expenses, Leslie concluded that she would need to make $2,000 over the next two weeks or she would literally be "homeless." Not having citizenship or a job, this might prove to be a difficult task. A salaried position would be futile as it would be impossible to generate those funds in such a short period of time, but rather than give up, Leslie started diligently searching the classified ad section of the *Los Angeles Times* for anything that even resembled an answer to her dilemma. She found an intriguing advertisement about weightloss and nutrition sales that hinted of fast money, and since she had taken a few nutrition courses in school, she figured she might be "cut out for this kind of thing." Leslie answered the ad, met her "sponsor," and went to her first Herbalife "meeting."

With loud music, people clapping, people talking, people everywhere, Leslie thought it felt more like a religious revival than a sales meeting. "I was very turned off. And even though I liked the product, this just wasn't something I was interested in." She found a seat, but then decided she would rather not stay. Leslie made an attempt to get to the door, but her rather tall sponsor "was talking to some associates and his knees were blocking the aisle." Feeling a bit embarrassed about trying to make such a hasty exit, Leslie hesitantly sat back down and listened to the presentation. "Literally if my sponsor had not been so tall, I wouldn't be in the business." A number of people stood up and gave impressive testimonials about the products, boasting of successful weightloss programs, and demonstrating that this was indeed a credible endeavor. Then some of the distributors spoke, one of whom had previously been a checker at a grocery store and who was now earning $2,000 per month. That was the magic number, that was all Leslie needed to hear.

Simple mathematics told Leslie that it could be done. "I knew I could do at least what she was doing, and maybe if I worked twice as hard, I could make the same $2,000 in half the time." This was a very exciting proposition to Leslie, and it gave her the hope she needed not to give up. She invested her last $30 on a distributor kit, and began her quest for the funds with which to pay her bills. "I didn't have any long-term dreams at the time. I thought the products were great, I was more desperate than anything else, and I knew I had to make the money." Not knowing anyone in Los Angeles, Leslie sold or tried to sell her new products to anyone and everyone who would listen to her. A petite blonde, and shy by nature, the social interaction alone was a challenge for her. But Leslie believes that panic can be a powerful motivator, and when "you're broke and desperate, you will do things you wouldn't normally do."

Leslie did much more than merely survive, she triumphed. Her first check from Herbalife was just over $2,000. Not only did she pay her bills with a few dollars to spare, but she realized that there was a tremendous amount of potential for the future. It suddenly seemed possible that she would never have to rely on anyone else again, and considering how she had come to be in this position, Leslie found the freedom very appealing. She proceeded to build a substantial account base in Los Angeles, and seeing that the possibilities were compounding daily, Leslie decided to take it one step further. She approached Mark Hughes, the president of Herbalife International with a suggestion of expanding the North American sales into Canada, and offered to "move back home and start selling." He agreed, and back she went.

By the time she had established herself in Canada, the number of products being sold and distributors being recruited was reaching astonishing proportions. At the end of the second month in her new territory she received a check for $8,400, and after only three months, Leslie was shocked to find a check in her mailbox for $19,500. "I ran to the bank to cash it because I was sure there must have been some mistake." It was no mistake, this was really happening. Leslie made $60,000 her first year in sales, and reached millionaire status only five years later at the age of 27. Now her income consistently surpasses $100,000 per month, and she receives residual income from distributors in 27 countries worldwide. Leslie seems just as surprised as anyone about the outrageous numbers generated by her sales, but she believes in the system, is committed to working hard, and believes in her product. "It's simple. Strive to get results with the product, tell others about those results, and work hard."

It may be a simple equation, but it is not always a bed of roses. "It's the most difficult to get past the cynicism," Leslie says. "You show them what you have and hope they believe through the product itself. But sometimes I have to show them a copy of my checks, and I don't like that." It would seem to those on the outside that some people in this business have a tendency to make money the absolute focus and a barometer for success. That is a problem for Leslie. "People say that money isn't everything, but it can be when you don't have anything," she says in defense of how she started. But even in light of her success, Leslie keeps working hard. "You have to make hay when the sun shines, and if I help enough people get what they want, I get what I want. It's a win-win situation." Admittedly now, she could certainly choose not to work as hard, but she still maintains that somewhere in the back of her mind a small source of motivation comes from the "ever present fear of being broke, and that it might all be gone tomorrow."

Contrary to popular belief, success in multilevel marketing doesn't "just happen," and sales skills, business skills, and people skills play fundamental roles in developing a profitable future. Nonetheless, a problem remains because most anyone who gets involved in this kind of work is an independent distributor, and most have essentially no background experience in business at all. Leslie thinks that people "can educate themselves about the products, and that's not difficult because most customers don't want anything technical, they just want to know if it works and how much it will cost." There are three distinct aspects to this business: marketing the products, building an organization and teaching distributors how to duplicate the process. As with any other product, results sell, and this is no exception.

"It is vital to your business that you personally use the products. It is your results and the results others see that will be the key to your retail success. In terms of building your organization, people will be attracted to the financial results they see you and others experience. In turn, you can teach them to create their own results and thereby duplicate the process." She also emphasizes follow-up skills, because at Herbalife the most substantial source of retail business emanates from repeat customers.

The sales aspect in multilevel marketing is fairly uncomplicated. It is basically a numbers game, and your success in selling hinges directly on your ability to contact people—lots of people. In the purest form, effort will be proportional to reward. "The more people you expose yourself to, the more chances you have of selling." The beauty lies in the notion that there are no limits. The target market is people who want to change their lives, and in today's world, there are certainly plenty of them. Many times she comes up against the cynics, but finds it best not to even attempt to argue with them, period. "You have to accept that people are very opinionated about this kind of thing." To make the approach less intimidating, Leslie chooses to use a sales style that is more "telling than selling," and her accomplishments alone sell themselves. Leslie suggests that just listening to others will present opportunities. "So many people can't stand their jobs, and everyone needs extra money." Leslie feels there is virtually "no such thing as job security anymore," so when people mention their predicament, Leslie offers a solution. She offers them their own job security.

She tells her associates that they need to concentrate on the things that actually provide them a return, i.e. "don't sort paper clips!". She has learned to delegate and refers to a Canadian saying "shoot the wolf nearest the sleigh" when she reflects on her own work ethic.

The simplest answer, however, may just be a matter of effort and determination. Leslie suggests working with complete focus on the task at hand. But Leslie still sees many people "work hard and still not make any money." She knows they are "busy" all day, but they do not accomplish anything that will actually make them money. For example, "they put together flyers, design ad campaigns and devise ways to get business, all the while they aren't spending any real time doing the things necessary to put cash in their pockets. Their hard work is misdirected." Leslie's advice is to try to resist getting wrapped up in strategies, but instead, make all working hours as productive as possible. Learning to employ yourself effectively is key in this kind of work. At the end of the day it is always important to ask the question, "Would I have been fired today if I worked for someone else?" As an independent sales entity, Leslie enjoys the idea that she can work where and when she pleases, and that there is no direct competition between distributors. She refers to herself as "laid back and low key," and finds a great deal of pleasure in the fact that she does not "have to be pushy because there are enough prospects for everyone." Leslie also understands not to rule anyone out as a potential recruit. "I've learned there is no way to judge who will be good and who won't. Some of the people I thought would do great bombed miserably, and some of the ones I thought were complete flakes turned out to be great distributors."

And the "great distributors" Leslie has recruited have in turn made her into one of the top five distributors in the world for Herbalife. The money is almost incomprehensible to most of us, but she seems to have remained very grounded and sincere regardless of her financial comfort. "The only thing money does is make you more of what you are. If you are a fool, you'll be a fool with money, and if you are generous, you'll be able to be even more generous." Once you have attained the level of monetary success she has, the focus inevitably has to change. Part of the reason Leslie continues to put in such long hours is because she feels a responsibility to so many people. "I'm very much aware that many people work hard and never get the financial rewards that I have. I feel very blessed in this way and feel compelled to help others." Even though there are times when Leslie feels frustration about when to say no, she is still very thankful for what she has. It's reassuring to see that her wealth isn't taken for granted and that her true compassion continually shines through. To Leslie, the most valuable gift she can give is her time.

Time is a huge issue in Leslie's world. Juggling work with three children and a husband can be a tall order to fill. She admits there is a constant struggle for balance between work and personal life. "When you're broke you do what you have to do to make ends meet, usually without regard for balance." As

Leslie has began to make money she was afforded what she calls "the opportunity to be more philosophical." " I can now afford to reflect. No one ever looked back on their life and wished they had spent more time at the office! I had to adjust my life accordingly."

You can form any opinion you would like about multilevel marketing, but Leslie's success shows it to be a credible and certainly viable industry. In the spirit of genuine entrepreneurialism, the sky is indeed the limit for Leslie Stanford at Herbalife International. She has proven that on a clear day you really can see forever.

To Leslie, the secret of success is: "To be in a constant state of awareness of opportunities to promote your business and your product. I never meet anyone or go anywhere without keeping my eyes open for possibilities."

• • • • • • • •

Leslie Stanford's personal vision of greatness:

"Great people and people I respect are people who have accomplished what they wanted in their life without having to compromise their integrity or their personal standard of right and wrong. That is what I strive for. If I can get to that point in my life, that would be great."

Where is Leslie now?

Leslie is still amongst the top Herbalife distributors in the world and plans to stay there!

THE PSYCHOLOGIST

"People are generally better persuaded by the reasons which they themselves discovered than by those which have come into the mind from others."

Pascal
Pensees (1670)

The Psychologist

Psychology is the science of dealing with the mind and mental processes, feelings, and desires. Utilizing psychology to examine below the surface of a given situation often reveals interesting insights, and the observation of certain aspects of body language and facial expressions can speak more strongly than words. It is often difficult and complicated to uncover the reasoning behind particular thoughts and motivations, and even more complex to draw logical and applicable conclusions as to their origin. Psychological analysis is more than an academic skill, it is a very special gift, and Mark Moskowitz has been endowed with it. A $30 million a year, top-rated residential real estate producer for Realty Executives, Mark has proven that psychology and sales make for a winning combination.

This native New Yorker, born in Brooklyn and raised in Long Island, maintains the formality of his eastern character. Even in Phoenix's scorching 110 degree weather, you'll find Mark in a crisp shirt and a tie. A distinguishing New York influence is recognizable in his voice, and he is always the eloquent professional. Looking far younger than his years, Mark is a gregarious, expressive extrovert. There is a certain familiarity about him that makes you feel as though you've just struck up a conversation with an old friend, and he is quite comfortable with discussions on any topic. But, beneath the surface is a much deeper individual. His attentive gaze is transfixed in one place just a fraction of a second longer than to be expected, permitting him that extra moment he needs to size up the situation at hand. Instinctive, intuitive, and usually directly on target, Mark employs everything he knows about psychology to his advantage.

From the time he was a very young man, Mark has been an inquisitive and aggressive thinker. Though the "greaser" in high school complete with "huge pompadour hair and a leather jacket," he recalls being particularly interested in courses like Chemistry and Physics. His choice for college was the prestigious C.W. Post College, a part of Long Island University. Mark's diverse interests led him in several directions while looking down the career path, but he finally directed his focus on psychology and was striving to obtain a degree in that field. Mark had hopes of entering the work force as a psychologist and began his endeavors specializing in cognitive psychology. At 23 years of age Mark was buried in his studies and things seemed to be headed in the right direction for his future.

Meanwhile, Mark's parents were busy planning a move to sunny Arizona where his father was aspiring to start a furniture manufacturing business. Mark agreed to take a couple of weeks sabbatical from school to help out, but as soon as he arrived in Phoenix, he knew this was where he wanted to stay. Mark literally never went back, he never even sent for his clothes! Moving to Arizona in 1972 would prove to be an indisputably good decision. Being unsure where the psychology element would fit in, Mark thought it best to set his sights on business. Despite not being exactly a sensation at the outset, Mark's first sales job laid the foundation for his future success.

In the early seventies, Mark was comparatively new in town and seeking employment. The health club craze was just beginning to accelerate, and Mark found an opportunity in area of membership sales at the International Health Spa. The sales methods generally taught in the health club industry were aggressive and very structured. "They threw me in with the experienced and effective salespeople and it was either sink or swim." Nonetheless, it was a valuable learning experience, and Mark credits the tough training for part of his later success. By observing his fellow sales representatives, he often saw a "relentless hard sell." Even though it achieved effective results, it was not the way Mark felt comfortable selling. Taking bits and pieces of what he saw around him, he was able to find a way to apply basic salesmanship skills and combine them with his insight to human behavior. The result—his own unique style.

Eventually, Mark became an extremely impressive membership salesman. His combined knowledge of psychology and the study of body language created the perfect background for selling. He generated the kind of positive energy that made his clients comfortable, and all the while his sales successes continued to escalate. A significant number of professional people came through the doors of the International Health Spa, so Mark was exposed to a wide spectrum of business people. As he became acquainted with his customers, he discovered that he was selling memberships to some very successful people in a number of different fields. He was surprised to hear them say, "You're smooth, you know what you are doing, you're sincere, maybe you should try something more lucrative." This was encouraging and appealing to Mark, and he began to give the options some further thought. Several of his best customers were in real estate, and repeatedly he would hear them say, "You would be good in the real estate world, you have what it takes, think about it." Knowing it might be time for a change, Mark did think about it.

Armed with the benefits of learning some tremendously important lessons, Mark decided to leave the spa business. Real estate had been the hot topic at the spa, and "enough people had said I'd be good at it, so I thought I would give it a try." Mark went through the interview process with Coldwell Banker which included a very intense two-day personality test. He accepted the position, but after a closer look, did not feel comfortable with the commission structure outlined for new realtors. "It just didn't make financial sense." So he backed away from the offer. Mark returned to the drawing board in search of a position that better suited his needs. He finally joined Red Carpet Realty in 1974, and one of the most successful careers in residential real estate had begun.

Mark stayed with Red Carpet for the next five years, and launched himself on a voyage of gaining knowledge and experience that would mold and solidify his individual style of selling. Real estate training certainly differed from the training at the health spa, most importantly because there essentially had been none. "My broker took me out and dropped me off in the middle of a neighborhood and told me to knock on about 200 doors and that he would pick me up in about three hours. I was standing there saying 'but...but...but...' and that was my sales training." Mark confesses with a smile that he actually had a reasonable amount of success with the endeavor. This "less than structured" training approach isn't reserved for particular companies, it is indicative of the real estate industry itself. "The difficulty comes with preparing a structure and sticking to it, because whatever structure this business has is the structure you create." Mark is extremely self-disciplined and has never let the freedom of approach interfere with work. "People sometimes think that realtors go out in the backyard to the money tree and pick off the money, and it's that easy. Regardless of the freedom, people don't realize that people work harder in real estate than in most other professions."

In 1979, Mark teamed up with a fellow realtor, Bill Powers, and the two of them struck out on their own. Mark described himself at the time as a "New Yorker with long hair that looked like a lion, with a full mustache," and his partner as " the native Arizona guy with short, short, hair and clean shave." He admits they were complete opposites, a bit of an "odd couple," but fast friends. They formed a company known as Home Brokers, and went forward with lofty hopes of having a significant bearing on the market. Timing is everything, and this was a trying period for business in general. The company grew to encompass a staff of 60 people, but the recession rendered it very exhausting to try to get people motivated. "Where there was usually 100 *"no"* answers for every one *"yes,"* it was more like 250 *"no"* answers for every one *"yes"* ." Mark and Bill were constantly struggling, and the bleakness of the future was looming rather ominously on the horizon.

Toward the end, Mark did everything he could to reorganize Home Brokers. He changed the commission structure, but was still left with below-average producers to cover the overhead. No amount of dedication seemed to be enough, and in 1982 they agreed to sell their business. Bill Powers went directly to Realty Executives where he is now the CEO and Vice President of Realty Executives International. Mark took a detour and found himself at a reputable Phoenix company called Ed Post Realty. He was exactly back where he started and remembers it as the lowest point in his career. "I did not have any clients to talk to. I was in a new area. I might as well have moved to Bolivia." Shortly after his arrival, Ed Post was sold to Coldwell Banker, and Mark was transferred into management. He wasn't overly excited about this prospect either. "The problem with being a manager was being confined to one place. I remember wearing a hole in the carpet that had a circular floor plan from just walking around and around. I felt like a caged animal. Not that it was a bad job, I just felt like my calling was to get out and sell." Nine months later that call finally came, and Mark started as an agent for Realty Executives.

By 1984, Mark had been named to the President's Round Table, a group comprised of the top 30 agents in Phoenix based on commission, regardless of company affiliation. He maintained this honor for the next five years, and by 1992 was not only Realty Executive's number one agent for the state, but the nation as well. In 1993, the distinction continued, naming Mark again as the top producer in Arizona, while placing him second overall in the nation. The year 1994 brought even more accolades for Mark, naming him Arizona's finest agent for a third consecutive year, and this time moving into the number one position in the United States, Canada and Mexico. The progressively upward trend in Mark's growth curve continues. For the last five years, Mark has consistently been ranked number one, two, or three worldwide for Realty Executives. And though it was a tedious struggle to reach this pinnacle of success, Mark plans on always being one of the best.

Real estate is a unique and highly competitive business, but Mark believes there are ways to be a standout and maintain high levels of success. First and foremost is understanding the market. "In real estate, everyone has access to the same information so the only thing that someone judges you on is your product knowledge and credibility." When Mark hires a new agent for his team, he will not permit them to see a client for the first 30 days. He suggests they choose homes in a price range where they feel comfortable, and then sends them out to see every house available in that same range. Once they begin to get listings, it is time to sharpen the business skills and concentrate on selling. "A big challenge for realtors is not only staying on top of existing transactions and to continue developing new business, but also to care for your current customer so that your standard of service does not decline."

The business aspect of real estate is very important to Mark. He admits that with the number of listings escalating so quickly, he was lacking in follow-up skills with his existing clients. Mark hired some people to "cover" this area because he never wanted to hear someone say, "Moskowitz, I remember you.

Didn't you list my house two months ago and I never heard from you again?" He now employs three licensed assistants who maintain customer service, coordinate transactions, and provide solid support in the day to day operations. Mark wanted to demonstrate to his clients that he was more than a salesman, but that he was a businessman as well. "I've seen a guy make 25 bona fide phone calls to sell a house, but he never makes the 26th call which should be to the owner to tell them what he's doing. We are in a results-oriented business whereby if I don't bring you an offer on your house, how do you know I'm not playing golf all day?" Customer service and keeping clients well informed has become a priority for Mark, and it has made a substantial difference to his work and his reputation.

For Mark, reputation is an integral part of being a good realtor. "I realize that yes, it's important for people to like you, but in order for you to gain their respect, you must have ethics for your foundation, provide strong customer service, and care about your customer throughout the entire transaction." When it comes to interacting with people directly, Mark is at his very best. He has true charisma, and an almost electrifying impact on everyone he meets. Beneath his genuine warmth lies an avid and attentive listener who puts his client's needs first. His contention is that "60 to 70 percent of most people are pretty much alike, and if you can appeal to the majority of people, you can substantially increase your chances of success." One of the ways Mark gets the job done is understanding how people think. "I feel people don't like to be told what to do, but if you tell them a parable, an Aesop's fable, or a story that happened to someone else and the consequences of that situation, then they can apply it to themselves and gain new perspective." Mark considers his story-telling skills to be one of his biggest strengths. By providing insights in this way, it allows them to draw their own conclusions, and they usually decide to finalize the transaction.

Behavioral psychology taught Mark that people can really learn anything they want to if they "come in as a blank slate with no preconceived notions," and this is undeniably applicable with salespeople. Mark feels that they can improve themselves and change their patterns by paying more attention to behavior. He admits that "a salesperson only has control of where the sales process is: beginning, middle or end. They never have control of someone's behavior, nor should they try. The trick is to try to adapt to that behavior in a wide range and lead it into a sale." Mark does not feel that selling has an interrelation with being smart, but instead with being intuitive and empathetic. "Real estate is an emotional sale coupled with a hard sale, so you have to be careful that people don't feel like they are being pushed." To Mark, it isn't that difficult to make an impact on people. He thinks they are impressed with the basics—humility, knowledge, and sincerity. Mark will never compromise the ethics of real estate, he wants to look in the mirror and "be proud of who he sees."

But all the humility, knowledge, and sincerity in the world will not alter the fact that real estate is normally an impassioned purchase, and one has to sell it that way. To really impact emotions, Mark says you have to set up a house in a specific way to accomplish what you want because "people don't remember what they see, they remember what they feel." That's why a very important part of Mark's sales presentation is staging. "Decorating a house for Architectural Digest or decorating a house for beauty are totally different than decorating a house for a sale. It's kind of like Dustin Hoffman in a western. He's 5'5" so they make the door 5'6". You have to give the best impression of the house that you can." Mark has made staging a form of art. He is able to create excitement about every room, and is meticulous about his "props" right down to the lighting. "People can only mentally move into the space you leave them," so Mark constructs an illusion that enables the home to be viewed in the best possible way. By doing this, the customer is able to feel the freedom to visualize themselves in the home. And more often than not, these illusions become a reality, and Mark adds another name to his long list of satisfied customers.

"It's funny, but I never aspired to be the top person in my company." Mark has never felt that money was going to "make or break" him, he just wanted to have enough to live the lifestyle he had chosen. He doesn't deny that it is a motivator, but feels it is fairly far down the list. "Being part of a successful group is more important than money, recognition is more important than money, responsibilities can be more important than money, even titles can be. But money is how we keep score." And though Mark's monetary rewards are unquestionably fulfilling, the real compensation for him is the effect each sale has on people's lives. "The three primary needs in life are food, clothing and shelter. I provide shelter. The joy and gratification of finding someone a home they love is very fulfilling."

Business and pleasure are synonymous to Mark. Real estate and his wife are his true passions. Jet, Mark's wife of 16 years, is also his partner and he is proud to say that they are "married to their work." He has also been known to hit a few golf balls, or swing a tennis racket from time to time, but Mark is quite content just putting in a full day of work. However you analyze it, every full day of work pays off and gives Mark an indisputable edge. And whether the psychological influences in his sales are real or imaginary, they do not create salespeople much better than Mark Moskowitz.

To Mark, the secret of success is: "Loving what I do to the extent that it becomes a passion. Knowing everything possible about all contracts, documents or other printed forms within the industry and securing knowledge of my product in all different price ranges both active on the market and properties already closed. And, always taking pride in being a professional."

• • • • • • • •

Mark Moskowitz's personal vision of greatness:

"I want to have inner peace. I want to be comfortable with myself and not have my success measured in terms of money. I want to enjoy my life."

Where is Mark now?

Mark remains one of the top brokers for Realty Executives both nationally and internationally. Though his personal success continues to climb, he has become completely focused on establishing the essence of "teamwork" in real estate. Mark has merged into a selling group with three other qualified and very talented agents. Their combined sales figures will exceed $70 million in one year. Mark's goal has always been to provide the ultimate in service, and he feels that a team atmosphere will provide his client base with the most complete and personal attention possible.

The Comedian

"The people you like when you meet them and while you know them, and the people you remember fondly, are invariably people who have a sense of comedy, not just a sense of humor."

William Saroyan
Chance Meetings
(1978)

THE COMEDIAN

Some people believe that it takes a certain sense of humor to succeed in sales. Some people also believe that it doesn't hurt to know a bit of juggling and magic too. Alan Fendrick, former stand-up comic and street entertainer, is one of those unique personalities who discovered very early that performing is in essence the most difficult kind of selling—a selling of yourself. And though you won't find Alan's name in lights on any marquee, he certainly achieved stardom within the competitive world of selling computers and computer related services.

I discovered Alan while reading a book about his company entitled *"How To Make A Buck And Still Be A Decent Human Being: A Week with Rick Rose at Dataflex."* The book was about "the sales and marketing strategies that catapulted Dataflex into the top 100 best small companies in America," and had discussed the accomplishments and astonishing sales figures of their top salesman at the time, Alan Fendrick. The information proved that Alan was a standout in more ways than one. He was described as "tall and gangly with brown hair that is only controllable through frequent haircuts," and it said his claim to fame was making an appearance on "The David Letterman Show." There was little doubt that he would be interesting to meet. It turns out that his special talent didn't exactly land him on David Letterman's guest list, but rather on the less than notable segment called "stupid human tricks." Not only can Alan sell an average of $15 million worth of computers and services annually, but he can also jump on a pogo stick while juggling two tennis balls and an apple, and recite the names of all the presidents in order from Washington to Reagan in the process! Hard not to consider this performance impressive.

Alan sounded light and funny on the phone. He seemed flattered by the entire prospect of my book and agreed to participate. This was my first interview, so in retrospect he was used as a kind of guinea pig for this whole process. Alan was of course very prompt in returning his cassette containing answers to my questionnaire. So with walkman in hand, my "get to know Alan Fendrick" hike began.

It becomes evident immediately that this man is very comfortable talking openly about himself. If you didn't know his profession you might be fooled into thinking you were talking to a well-rehearsed entertainer. His answers are filled with comic undertones (which he refers to as "digressions into attempted humor"), and he is obviously enjoying himself. Alan, a first-generation American on his mother's side, married with a wife and two sons, speaks with pride about his family. He is inspired by his Polish-born mother, a survivor of the Holocaust, social worker, and an over-achiever who went back to school at the age of 50 to earn her Master's Degree. His father, always showing Alan the value of hard work, is an accountant from Scranton, Pennsylvania. Alan sounds much older, and definitely much wiser than his actual age. He comes across very likeable, intelligent, and his quick wit adds to his story telling skills. As the tape winds on, Alan casts that certain kind of spell usually reserved for motivational speakers. His words flow easily in a captivating tone that allows people to listen for hours and hours and not really notice the passage of any time. Meeting him in person was certainly going to be a treat.

Since the weather at the time was miserable on the east coast, it was mutually agreed that Alan would fly to Phoenix. This wasn't exactly a difficult sell considering the extra bonus of golf and sunshine! A dinner was scheduled with a small group of my associates, and I arrived early to make sure everything was perfect for my first meeting with this computer whiz-kid. Having formulated a picture of him from a voice, it was a bit of a surprise when I was able to tangibly put the two together. Yes, he was tall. Gangly was a bit of an overstatement, but the hair description was right on target. Dressed in a pressed rugby shirt and jeans (which I would later discover was his personal uniform), Alan Fendrick looks to be the walking definition of a preppie fraternity boy. He seems twenty-three on a stretch (not at all thirty), all smiles, and not a care in the world. Perhaps the fact that he had sold a record $32 million in computer hardware that year lent to his demeanor. But as I came to know Alan, I discovered that it wasn't always "happy-go-lucky" for this young success story.

Alan grew up in Mount Laurel, New Jersey. It was there he had his first experience with sales while delivering newspapers and selling subscriptions to his hometown daily *The Laurelite.* A natural salesman even as a child, Alan recalls learning two valuable life lessons from this early work: "Sell only to the decision maker, and when the sale is made, keep your mouth shut!" He was considered a fairly undistinguished high school student with a "B" average. Not exactly an over-achiever at the time, Alan managed to rise to the occasion and come up with sufficient S.A.T. scores to get himself accepted to Rutgers University in New Jersey. Listening to his rapid-fire speech and wide range of knowledge, Alan's intellect is never in question. Having a double major in Economics and Political Science with a minor in Computer Science, he seems to epitomize the book-smart student. But as always, looks can be deceiving!

"The years I learned about life." That is how Alan remembers his four years in college. He felt he was very immature while going to school, and though not much for formal classroom education, he is convinced that he is more worldly for the experience. To say Alan is opinionated would be putting it lightly and convincing him that someone else's views are valid might not be an easy task. Nonetheless, he is sure that his exposure to so many kinds of people in college tempered that attitude enough to help him respect other people's viewpoints—even if he didn't agree with them. Alan feels there is a "tremendous amount of pressure placed upon students to finish college" for the reason that success is so often equated with an education. Despite four years of hard work, Alan never completed his degree and has no problem sharing this with you. In fact, he wears it as a personal badge of honor to demonstrate to the world that it is possible to succeed without a diploma. Alan is like a human sponge when it comes to learning. He has an incredible amount of energy, listens intently and always asks questions. When you talk to Alan you invariably have to be thinking a step ahead, for if you do not, you're bound to get left behind. The most prevalent word in his vocabulary is "why," and he can get a bit pushy if you don't have an answer that suits him. His intellect is a definite strong point, but his most powerful attribute remains his sense of humor.

Whether it be on the phone, in front of a group, or one on one with a client, Alan Fendrick is a funny man. He is animated, electric and his comedic talent, in a roundabout way, is the very reason Alan ended up in sales in the first place. During college, Alan discovered that he had a real knack for making people laugh, and felt fairly confident that comedy was to be his career. He was doing a combination stand-up, magic and juggling act at some less than memorable clubs around Philadelphia and New York, learning quickly that show business is a much more tedious endeavor than it appears. He has the ultimate respect for comics who have "made it" because he knows how difficult it really is to succeed in that business. Money at the bottom of the comedy chain was nothing to speak of, and his limited performances were hardly earning him enough to make ends meet. Deciding that he could no longer suffer for his art, Alan took up a job bartending to supplement his income.

The bartending work was far from glamorous, but it exposed Alan to a lot of interesting people in addition to giving him a daily venue to showcase his talents. One day while at the bar, some business men came in and mentioned that they were in need of a magician/bartender to work on a cruise they were sponsoring for their associates. Always in search of extra cash, Alan was quick to say yes. The cruise went well, Alan was a smash hit, everyone had a great time, and then it was back to tending bar. About a week later, the president of the company that had sponsored the cruise called Alan and told him he would like to speak to him about a future with the company. Not taking this idea too seriously, and not being too sure where his career path was leading, Alan agreed to hear what the man had to say. Much to Alan's surprise, he was offered a sales job right then and there. As is his style, Alan wanted to make sure that he hadn't misrepresented himself to this man or his company. He was careful to explain that he "didn't have a college degree, had been working as a bartender for the past year and a half, and had virtually no sales experience." The man understood Alan's background perfectly and told him the company wanted to "hire a personality," and the training would follow. The comedy career was dying a slow death, but Alan knew his "personality" would pull him through, and so that day "Alan the salesman" was born.

It didn't take long for our rather sharp newborn to realize that his new employer wasn't exactly the most savvy of businessmen. The limited business knowledge Alan had gleaned from college offered him enough insight to see that this company was being run directly into the ground. Nonetheless, the experience was valuable, and Alan was afforded the opportunity to learn the inner workings of a very small company. After six long months of giving it his best, Alan was off on his first real vacation. A week in Jamaica left him tan and rested, yet he wasn't exactly prepared for what had transpired while he was away.

Alan returned to find his fellow employees staring blankly at a yellow "police" tape across the front of the office space. "It looked like something you would see on one of those bad television cop shows!" He and his associates were ushered into what was left of a room in the now burned up building, and given a vague explanation as to what had occurred. Seems the president of the company (the same man who had hired Alan) slipped over the edge of reason after realizing that the company was facing financial ruin and had set fire to the entire place. Needless to say, Alan's short sales career had suddenly gone up in smoke, and he was once again seeking employment.

A fellow victim of the fire fiasco told Alan about a company down the street called Dataflex that was hiring salespeople. Anxious to work again, Alan gave them a call. He eagerly explained his sales background, experience, and desire to work for their company, but to no avail. He was given a curt "thank you, but we are not interested." Alan is a fighter, and not particularly skilled at taking "no" for an answer. He agrees that some may consider his behavior to border on the obnoxious, but he usually gets what he wants. And when it came to Dataflex, an interview was what he wanted more than anything. Years of struggling as a comedian had taught Alan not only to survive, but to apply 100% of himself all the time. He was determined to get this job whether he was qualified for it or not. Maybe Alan wasn't exactly what they were looking for, but it is very difficult to change Alan's mind once it has a goal to achieve.

Suffice to say, the goal was reached. Alan did obtain an interview, and Dataflex found themselves with one of the finest computer hardware and service salesmen in the country. He was the 42nd person hired at this growing company, whose staff expanded to as high as 1600 while he was in their employ. The average salesperson in the computer industry produces about a million to a million and half dollars a year in sales. Dataflex had a sales force who generate hundreds of millions in revenue for the company, and Alan managed to stay at the top of that pack. In his best year, Alan sold $36 million and averaged $15 million a year in hardware sales throughout his career. During his last two years at Dataflex, his focus expanded to selling services and support, and in that area alone he recorded $5 million a year in sales, versus the industry average of closer to $600 thousand in a year. In his last month with the company, Alan broke personal records by billing over $500 thousand in sales in one month.

Alan credits much of his success to the training he received at Dataflex. He feels that too many salespeople "simply don't take the time to really understand their industry, let alone their own company." He discovered there is an important difference between someone teaching you something, and someone allowing you to learn. "Teaching is spoonfeeding, learning takes some thought." Asking questions, questions and more questions seems to be Alan's strategy. He is quick to warn, "there is no such thing as a stupid question and the only way to learn is simply to ask." Alan believes that the root of all evil in sales is to be solely motivated by money. Admittedly it is difficult to avoid, but "if you let that obsession take the place of sound thinking, it may eventually be your downfall."

When it comes to sales, Alan feels his best attributes are his sense of humor, his persistence, and his endless desire to learn. He reads everything pertinent to his career, and always tries to pick up a couple of ideas he can apply not only to his business, but to his own life. He recalls a lesson he learned when he was just starting out as a magician that has stayed with him and remained applicable throughout his career. "An older, more experienced magician told me that one of the biggest mistakes an amateur magician makes is to buy packaged tricks or gimmicks from a catalog or magic store. The real key is to learn sleight of hand. And the only way to learn sleight of hand is to buy the books, study them, and keep trying until you get it right. I thought the books were too expensive so I kept trying the gimmicks, and was just like everyone else. The older magician kept telling me to buy the books, and they will pay for themselves." Finally Alan bought the books, and boasts that he mastered sleight of hand, and more importantly learned to be a magician, rather than a guy who just does tricks. "It's the same with sales," Alan says, "if you use the gimmicks, you're just like everyone else."

Some salespeople have built up emotional walls to protect themselves from the rejection that inevitably comes with their careers. But Alan is a very emotional man, and not embarrassed to share that. He used to be shy about those kinds of things, but now says he "will let people know him as much as they want to." He also knows his limits and isn't afraid to ask for help when he needs it. "I know what I'm good at, and what I'm not." Alan's motto is to "understand what my clients want and show them how I can help them get it." Alan wants to be the guy who will do the things other people don't want to do, the guy that finds the line and then crosses it. "I make it a point to keep drawing and moving that line and just say the things

I'm thinking, period." To him, sacrifice and pain are interchangeable and they are a part of every salesperson's life. He looks you straight in the eye with conviction when he reminds you that "you simply cannot get comfortable in a sale, because if you get comfortable, you are going backwards."

Selling is believing, and if Alan believes in something he can sell it. "If I truly believe in my product and tell enough people about it, I'll get my share of the business." But it isn't always an easy equation, even for those who are very good at it. Alan agrees that his rejection rate is high, as in all sales, which "leaves a lot of room for improvement." The toughest thing for him seems to be getting people who are already unhappy to change. Finding a source of motivation to initiate that change is Alan's biggest challenge. But when asked how to do that, there was no set answer. "It's the sum of parts," Alan contends, "personality, background, family, love for money. Sometimes you just have to draw on whatever you have to make the sale, and most of the time that means listening to yourself talk and really hearing what you have to say." But no matter what Alan may come up with, he always holds tight to his notion that honesty is a constant. "Be honest with yourself, and be honest with your client."

With technology advancing at what seems to be the speed of light, business in general is an extremely competitive place. Alan refers to it as "an arena that's changing so rapidly. One of the biggest value adds I can bring to my client is just keeping current." In order to stay one step ahead of the game, Alan tries to visualize situations and anticipate the needs of his customers. "You must learn to trust your intuition, and keep it clear in your head that intuition is an absolute necessity in your success." For example, on the phone, Alan tries to get a feel for the person rather than just receive information. "You have to be more intuitive and commanding on the phone than in person. You don't have the physical things when you're on the phone like looks, a smile, a handshake, the props. You only have your voice and the ability to listen." Though it has been a strong part of his sales philosophy, Alan admits that even the best intuitive instincts can be wrong. "Bad experiences remind me to go back to the basics. Basics are believing in yourself, believing in what you do, believing in your product, knowing your product well, and being able to communicate effectively. If you don't have product knowledge, you don't have a career."

Though some might consider Alan's methods a "hard sell," he feels it's beneficial to focus on the moment at hand and strike while the iron is hot. "Time is a salesperson's biggest enemy. The more time you leave, the more things can crop up. You should ask for the sale immediately. Asking for the sale up front can never jeopardize the final sale." But there is a fine line to walk with this approach, and Alan adds that "you want to be careful not to badger a client or question a client too much, you just want to get people to talk." And talk to Alan they will. Alan credits this to being himself and being an individual, and in the breadth of "selling," he believes that "true salespeople are not dependent upon their companies, they are dependent upon themselves as an entity."

If you look closely at successful people, you will see they not only work hard, but play hard as well. They are as passionate about their hobbies as they are about their work, and it has probably made them better salespeople. Alan is particularly fond of ping pong. He took up the sport when he was a freshman at Rutgers, whose team happened to be ranked number one in the country. At the top of his game, Alan was ranked 175th in the United States out of approximately 10,000 active tournament players. He still plays, and even competes on occasion. But his interest doesn't stop at ping pong balls; Alan is a huge sports fan, especially basketball. He calls Charles Barkley of the Houston Rockets his "hero" because "Charles is willing to say what is on his mind, without regard for what is politically correct or what might get him an endorsement."

When it's not sports, it's numbers. The stock market fascinates Alan, and he admits that he probably dabbles in it a bit more than he should. Most likely related to his love of money, Alan finds "the notion of making and losing fortunes" to be intriguing. At one time having had an office in the World Trade Center in New York City made it easy to get hooked, and occasionally Alan would go by and watch the traders on the floor. Staring down with eyes as big as saucers it's a wonder he didn't become a stockbroker instead!

Sports and numbers aside, magic is always a part of the magician. Alan still loves to show off his talents for his two young sons. Some of Alan's fellow stand-up comedians from the early eighties have managed to hit it big, and even though he has little spare time, he tries to keep up with them and all the latest stars in the clubs and on television.

Time and energy are precious commodities in this busy man's life, but he feels you have to either do it completely or not at all. Therefore, it's important to always have a source of inspiration, and for Alan, it's his children. He recalls some financial difficulties his parents had when he was growing up and he never wants his children to experience those kinds of hardships. Alan views life as an incredible learning experience and he thinks that people miss out on so much. "They live in this crazy world with constant pressure and no one takes the time to have fun." Alan knows he has the ability to make people smile and laugh, the money and success are just a bonus.

To Alan, the secret of success is: "Understanding what you really want out of life and working to get it. There's a difference between "working to get it" and "getting it." There is an old saying I subscribe to that success is a journey, not a destination. I think Jack Palance's character "Curly" (in the movie City Slickers) was right on target. Dedicate your life towards working hard for the thing(s) you want out of life, and you are a success."

• • • • • • • •

Alan Fendrick's personal vision of greatness:

"To have everyone who comes in contact with me enjoy the experience. It's simple because then I'll know that I'm accomplishing everything I want to do if I can accomplish that."

Where is Alan now?

Alan has developed, and continues to develop, new businesses. He currently owns a communications consulting firm called Millennium Consulting Council, Inc. and is a partner in an Internet business (Internet Directory Publishers - www.idpub.com) that helps small and mid-sized businesses to establish a strong Internet presence. He says "My ten years selling for Dataflex gave me an incredible opportunity to learn sales, and also business. I got to watch and be a part of a start-up company that made it to the dance floor. I apply this knowledge to my current business every day."

THE SPECIALIST

"The key to success isn't much good until one discovers the right lock to insert it in."

Tehyi Heieh
Chinese Epigrams Inside Out and Proverbs (1948)

THE SPECIALIST

There is a certain presence that surrounds athletes. Their stature, their demeanor, the way they carry themselves that shows others they believe they are good at what they do. They exude confidence. They have fine-tuned their bodies and minds to focus on one thing, and use that energy to perfect themselves within the sport they have chosen. Jim Richardson is an athlete. He mastered the game of basketball, and when injuries prevented him from pursuing it further, he conquered the game of baseball. He excelled in sports, he is fiercely competitive, a specialist. He always had to win. When the opportunity presented itself to get into the commercial real estate game, Jim Richardson took every ounce of his athletic ability, all of his sports-minded inner discipline and concentrated on challenging himself in a new arena. And again he triumphed. As an innovative leader and First Vice President of CB Commercial's Biosciences Group, with personal sales figures surpassing $50 million annually, and now senior acquisitions manager for a progressive equity company, Jim Richardson has proven that he can win at any game he plays.

Meeting Jim Richardson for the first time is an unsettling experience. He has an air about him that intimidates, and a stance that insinuates power. It's obvious from the moment you say hello that you are dealing with a man of purpose and perfection who will leave little room for those who fail to meet his expectations. After some time passes, and you become comfortable in his presence, you will discover that Jim does have a gentle side, complete with a warm smile and sense of humor. Nonetheless, lurking underneath is an ultra-competitive winner, a salesman with a high degree of intensity, and a man who feels comfortable being the number one player.

Our meeting begins with lunch. He volunteers to drive since he knows the area, and I find myself half expecting to see him in a flashy Porsche of some kind, or at very least an overstated Mercedes. Relieved, and to some extent impressed with his subtlety, I get into the passenger's side of a modest, but meticulously kept, 1985 BMW 535. We "break the ice" with some small talk, and then start moving towards the source of this dominating personality. Most of us are, to some degree, a reflection of our parents. We are, whether we admit it or not, a product of how we were raised. Jim is no exception. Growing up in southern California, he and his two brothers were brought up in a strict, but loving household. The Richardson home was very structured, but never lacking in the emotional support. He characterizes his mother as a woman with a "gentle demeanor and an absolute commitment to every facet of her sons' lives." Jim describes his father as a "very strong disciplinarian, a perfectionist, with rigid guidelines." He had what he calls a "healthy fear" of his father which instilled him with a respect for authority. Looking back, Jim didn't understand his father's methods, but now realizes the benefits of stern rules and knows that his personal and professional success can be attributed in part to this very same disciplined upbringing he sometimes resented. Jim credits both of his parents with a profoundly positive influence on his life.

Along with discipline, Jim's father had a tremendously strong work ethic, and 16 to 18 hour days were not unusual. In the printing business, not only was he a proprietor, but a salesman as well. Jim has less than fond memories of his father making him walk door-to-door to help develop sales for the business. "I was insecure enough as a teenager, I hated it!" But valuable lessons are always learned from taking the path we wouldn't have walked down without some prodding. It was a "character builder" for Jim, and the lesson taught was that "this kind of rejection was not the end of the world—even though it felt like it!" Jim never let it get the best of him, and worked for his father for 10 years throughout high school and college, but in the end never really saw it as a career choice. Though he loved business, sports were his passion, and he hoped it would be his future. Jim made it a point to pursue each game with emotion and a commitment to excellence, similar to the manner in which he now pursues his career.

A self-proclaimed "sports fanatic," Jim centered his energies around winning. He played all the major sports while in high school, but narrowed it down to basketball when he began his studies at Claremont Men's College. Jim's tall, athletic build made him a standout performer, but unfortunately a series of ankle injuries prevented him from reaching his own expectations. As is the trend with good athletes, he made a smooth transition into another sport. This time it was baseball. Again he was one of the best, and played baseball for the duration of his college career. Not to be overshadowed by his athletic prowess, Jim had equally impressive abilities as a student.

Majoring in Economics, Jim always had a firm grasp of the business world. His methodical thinking and intellect made facts and figures seem simple. To add to his education, Jim was exposed to his friends' parents, most of whom were business people, and quite a few who were involved with commercial real estate. Asking questions and being somewhat familiar with real estate in general piqued Jim's curiosity to pursue it further. He began to develop a "rudimentary understanding" of the different components of the industry, and wrote his senior thesis on "Mixed Land Use Development." But the sports issue still prevailed, and rather than go directly into the working world, Jim chose to play semi-professional baseball in Canada.

After a season, Jim returned to California. Having been home from Canada only a month, he had not quite sorted out where his life was heading, and found himself open to suggestions. Jim's wife was just getting ready to begin her own career as a stockbroker and very much wanted to stay in the San Francisco area. That all sounded fine, but it did not help make a career choice any easier. By chance, there was a 25th anniversary party for his in-laws in southern California. Jim and his wife attended and ran into a lot of people who were involved in California's explosive commercial real estate market. Having always had a strong yet undefined interest in this field, Jim listened intently to the possibilities. Someone at the party mentioned that there might be an opening at what was then known as Coldwell Banker (CB) in San Francisco, and the rest, as they say, is history.

CB Commercial is the largest commercial real estate company in the world. It is known for its high level of integrity, commitment to quality, and wide breadth of services. Jim fit right in. They offered extensive training programs designed to comprehensively educate their brokers in all aspects of the industry. Jim began what was known as the "wheel program" for his training, which put him in different offices serving different functions throughout the Bay Area in three-month increments. At the end of a year, he had to re-interview with those same respective offices, and when that process concluded, he would spend another 12 months under the tutelage of the one who had hired him directly. A complicated process, but a very effective program.

Most commercial brokers begin as generalists. They represent people on both sides of the fence, i.e. the people selling or leasing the buildings, and the parties looking to buy or lease them. Jim also began as a generalist, but he was market specific. His specialty was industrial, and he was responsible for basic industrial product brokerage in Central San Mateo County. Concentrating on an area seven miles long, two miles wide, Jim discovered early that specializing was the key to success. Though his knowledge was geographic, he made it a point to submerge himself in the area and uncover all he could about the companies he was servicing and what their specific needs were. What Jim discovered was an extremely high concentration of biotechnology companies with very distinctive real estate needs that were being overlooked by most brokers. He had found his niche; he had found his specialty.

At the forefront of carving out this niche was Jim's nearly obsessive desire to win. He knew he had tapped into a gold mine and was anxious to watch it materialize. In the early stages of his career, his co-workers described him as self-righteous, abrupt, and sometimes even obnoxious. Motivated by competition and the desire for money, Jim's "cut and dry" view of business developed him into a top contender. Though he was never driven to earn money purely as a means of obtaining material comforts, Jim did see his earnings as a measure of success relative to his peers. "Winning was everything." Regardless of the arena of competition, he was driven to come out on top. Jim recalls "taking losses very hard, generally being a poor loser." His overly competitive nature seemed to feed his definition of value for himself. " Winning and losing to a great extent defined my internal sense of worth." He admits, "I couldn't believe it when a prospective client would choose someone instead of me," but over time, "it becomes less important, there is plenty of opportunity for everyone." Jim's "black and white" state of mind created what he calls a "hard, judgmental edge," but he would like to think that he has softened as he has matured professionally and personally. Retrospectively, he attributes much of his attitude to general insecurity or low self-esteem which manifests itself into a performance-based mentality, but at the peak of his career this drive has served him well.

Sales, especially in high-ticket markets such as commercial real estate, has a tendency to create a "killer instinct." Jim believes that brokers become very self-important because "the amount of revenue you generate defines your value in this culture." It establishes a kind of hierarchy, and if you buy into it, you will find yourself being consumed by the greed and materialism. Since commercial brokers get paid on a total dollar volume basis, there are plenty of subtle ways to take advantage of clients to make money. Jim contends that "the longer you've been at it, the more success you have, the more variety and depth of opportunity you'll have, and the more trade-offs there will be." But if you want to make it in the long run, "you'll have to maintain your integrity and honor your commitments. Don't ever compromise your standards or sacrifice what's right."

It seems to be an ongoing battle to fight for the character of this profession as a whole. "Many people in this business are considered grossly overpaid," Jim says, and so it's up to the brokers to establish their value and prove differently. As a salesman involved with massive dollar transactions, he is constantly trying to "establish himself as a professional, and show his clients that they got their money's worth." Jim believes that "value added service" is an overused cliché that rings hollow with many clients. "To be a success in this business you must give clients something measurable." The new credo in corporate America is to do it better, faster, and cheaper. But in sales in the field of commercial real estate, where you are trying to sell a service as a product, you must concentrate on "delivering something tangible." Jim thinks the secret is to always "show them the end result, show them step by step what you are doing for them, don't be nebulous." He suggests if you want to validate yourself and the sale, use a "specific knowledge, a specific system, and a specific methodology."

This constant validation process drives Jim forward and motivates him to structure his business differently. He has gone beyond the traditional broker role of putting parties together and negotiating the transaction. He has geared himself toward a more "consultative approach," and focuses on helping the biotechnology companies he works with to develop strategic real estate plans that interact with their corporate business plans. Jim describes his prospects as "brilliant, process-driven people who require a continuous stream of evidence and validation consistent with their own research and development." So to meet their needs, and to evolve as a broker, one must always "see the trends, stay ahead of the trends, assist the trends, or try to adjust to them. Make your own work the prototype for what your company should be doing." There are constant structural changes going on in business, and it all impacts real estate and workplace environments. "It is as much an art as it is a science." Jim suggests that brokers learn to respond proactively to their specific market, however they may define it, and seize as many opportunities as they can during the up cycles as well as the down. If you do this, you are "insulated to a great extent against the inevitable market or industry fluctuations which are out of your control, and your long-term game plan should always be to continuously re-engineer yourself and your business. This is the best defense against broker burnout."

And there is inevitably a burnout phase in this game. Even the best of the best cannot maintain themselves at a high level of intensity for 15 or 20 years. "When you do burn out, you have to back down, reinvigorate yourself, get charged up and go in a new direction." Jim's direction is still strongly focused on the biotech market. He doesn't feel he has hit the burnout phase that he has seen so many brokers go through because he has become so highly specialized. "There are few brokers that are generalists that are hugely successful for an extended period of time." Jim has never spent time with the "blanket marketing" approach. "If you aren't market specific, the client cannot perceive the value of your services." He has educated himself so that he has a strong working knowledge of the biotech industry. Because of the unique requirements inherent to biotech companies, their facilities are two or three times more expensive to develop than traditional office buildings. Jim's dedication to learning the inner workings of this industry has paid off. "Because of my time investments, I have both a perceived and real advantage over my competitors."

Another edge for Jim is his ability to build the most important foundations in business: good relationships. Despite his intensity, Jim's genuine client advocacy attitude has been a tremendous tool in bridging the gap between broker and client. " I believe it is clear to my clients and co-workers that my relationship with them is more important than any transaction." He doesn't particularly enjoy or excel at initiating the relationship, but relishes the personal and professional rewards that result from "developing that bond into something special and unique whether it be long or short term." He does not believe one can separate his business and personal life, and it is permissible, even beneficial to let them get intertwined. It must be a working attitude because Jim has successfully obtained business from many of the most prominent and exciting biotechnology companies in the Bay Area and throughout the country. In 1994, Jim and his group brought in a combined total of $200 million in transactional volume for CB Commercial. And Jim's once three-person sales team has grown to include 25 people in 18 offices across the country.

During this skyrocketing pattern of growth in his business, along with unprecedented financial successes and accomplishments, Jim has undergone significant personal transitions as his professional career has evolved. He has become a more spiritual man, and credits his faith for the gradual, yet pronounced changes in his life. "The economic motivation or inspiration was fairly short-lived for me. It is now a by-product of my professional growth rather than the all consuming end." Jim's goals play a more subtle role in his life than they used to. "My goals have moved away from specific measurable criteria generally associated with economics to more subjective ones longer term in nature." His focus now is on team building, value enhancement and market share issues. Though maintaining a reputation for being meticulous, and sometimes extreme, Jim has learned to recognize that "there is only so much you can do, only so much you can expect. You have to realize that you and your compatriots are human." Probably a difficult embodiment for a man such as Jim, and he is finding out that old habits die hard. He still does not always see eye-to-eye with other people, he just doesn't make it so obvious!

Regardless of the changes Jim has made, he is still a high-strung sales executive who is trying to take the time to unwind. Outside of work, his energies are dedicated to his four children and his wife. Their spiritual growth as a family represents admirable work, and Jim is proud of the way their solid and unwavering faith has impacted their lives. Though still a "sports fanatic," Jim imparts most of his athletic talents through coaching various team sports for his young boys. And as for winning—it may not be the only thing, but has certainly been the best thing for Jim Richardson.

To Jim, the secret of success is: "To incorporate a variety of character traits and inherent skill sets including vision, focus, diligence, persistence, integrity, judgment, discernment, humility, and teamwork. However, the absolute essential ingredients are purpose and perspective. Without purpose one lacks the passion and motivation to succeed. Without perspective a balanced life and therefore successful life is unattainable."

• • • • • • • •

Jim Richardson's personal vision of greatness:

"First, to have a positive impact on the lives of people that are put in front of me each day. So many people from different walks of life and with different agendas are encountered on a daily basis. If I am able to establish a reputation for integrity, truth, wisdom and compassion, I will increasingly be presented with the opportunities to make a real impact in these people's lives. Second, to be a successful father and husband. To create a legacy for my children, and to have them be solid and good citizens."

Where is Jim now?

Jim has made a transition within his industry. With the help of a series of solid relationships built while at CB Commercial, Jim was offered a position with a prominent player in the biosciences field, Alexandria Real Estate Equities, Inc. headquartered in Pasadena, California. As one of the senior officers in the company, Jim has made an extremely successful transition from sales to management and leadership of a public company. Jim believes that "if you take a certain approach to servicing your clients, you will allow your salesmanship to transcend itself and other opportunities will present themselves that will broaden your perspective beyond pure sales."

The Rising Star

"To please people is a great step towards persuading them."

Lord Chesterfield
Letters To His Son (1739)

The Rising Star

On any given night, you can look up in the sky and see literally thousands of stars. So many in fact, that after awhile they all begin to look the same. Nonetheless, if you look closely enough you are bound to see one that shines brighter than the others, and it may even leave a glowing trail of fire as it shoots across the seemingly infinite galaxy. Those are the special stars, those are the ones you are certain to notice. Diane Donley is undeniably one of those stars. Working for Quebecor Printing, the second largest printing company in North America with a staff of over 18,000 worldwide, it would be easy to simply blend in and not definitively shine through. But Diane has an extraordinary ability to rise above the rest. Still in her twenties, having already been recognized as Salesperson of the Year, and generating personal sales figures surpassing $25 million, she is the most dazzling and radiant luminary in Quebecor's sky.

"Assertive, focused, but definitely not aggressive," is how Diane describes herself to me several times during our interview. But I'm not sure who she was trying to convince, me or her! And contrary to her steadfast definition, I would have a tendency to believe that in order to have achieved her kind of success in so little time, and within the confines of a huge corporation, there had to be at least a hint of aggressiveness involved! She says "No." I think "Hmmm." Regardless, this is not your average "girl out of college" getting her feet wet in the sales world. Diane is a businesswoman all the way through, with backbone, initiative, and enough gumption to ensure a rapid rise up the corporate ladder.

I was in a bit of a shambles the day I met Diane in Boston. My luggage had been lost in transfer from New York and I spent the afternoon walking the cobblestoned streets on tired feet searching for a change of clothes to purchase in hopes of looking half-way presentable for my meeting. Luckily, my baggage arrived in time, and I was able to make it to the hotel lobby to greet her with my composure intact. There is always much to be said for a solid first impression, and Diane certainly is exemplary in that capacity. This young yet sophisticated woman conveys such a strong essence of maturity and confidence that it seems unusual to consider that she is only in her mid-twenties. Diane is a professional to the point of being formal, so I thought it preferable to take her out of her element. We found ourselves at the Samuel Adams Brew Pub to help diminish the strain of her work day, and I quickly observed that even when her business persona is delegated to the back burner, this is still a very composed and dedicated young lady.

Born in San Jose, California, raised in Dallas, Texas, Diane's accent sounds suspiciously East Coast. Living in New England seems to befit her nicely, and she appropriately dresses the part in a perfectly tailored, sharp business suit. She is constantly making direct eye contact, and it is obvious that she is quite comfortable with herself. Diane has always been this way—the consummate over-achiever. A model student who held her first job at the age of 15, Diane was on the road to success very early. When she began college, her initial inclination was to become a veterinarian, but Diane only pursued that idea briefly before determining that she was at the wrong institution to pursue this type of career. From that decision, her thoughts turned to advertising. Still not entirely satisfied, she gave the business field a try. Not unlike most college students, being undecided was sounding like a viable option. Luckily, however, the business idea stuck. All the pieces began to fall into place, and Diane was convinced that this was the route to her future. She accomplished a double major, earning dual degrees in Marketing and International Business from the University of Texas at Austin. Maintaining a grade point average of 3.75, Diane completed the five-year study program in four years.

Even by her sophomore year in college, Diane had begun considering applying her knowledge to the working world. She took on a job in marketing support at a large business service center named NYNEX, a division of New York and New England Telecom, selling computers and networking systems. The exposure led Diane to believe that her career goal would eventually be within the technologies industry. At 19 years of age she was interfacing with sales representatives and learning the ins and outs of sales and service. Diane thought the "office environment taught professionalism and discipline," and she became exceedingly dedicated to her part-time position. She continued working with NYNEX during the next several semesters, and as graduation time drew near, the company extended her an offer of full-time employment. Nonetheless, she chose to keep her options open. The College of Business regularly hosted the attention of a number of extremely reputable corporations, and Diane's proven record was certain to hold her in good standing when serious interviewing commenced.

The summer prior to her senior year, coincidentally about the time the interview process was becoming a reality, Diane's parents moved to New England. Diane was invited to a golf outing with some family friends, and it was there that the possibilities available with Quebecor Printing began to interest her. She met up with some sales personnel employed by the company, and rather candidly asked them about what was at the forefront of her thoughts at the time, their income potential. "I was always kind of interested in money," Diane says with a smile, "I mean who wasn't at 19!" And though she had been extended a good offer from NYNEX, and had spoken to both Compaq and Apple Computer, the possibilities in the printing business presented some fresh appeal. She had the immediate impression that despite the massive size of the company, she could "really make some money," so she put them on her list of prospective interviews.

While in New England that same summer, Diane did complete a series of interviews at Quebecor. The work certainly had interesting possibilities, and the growth potential in terms of income was even more attractive. "To be honest, the most appealing aspect of sales in general was money." But the bottom line was that Diane had been determined to stay in the Dallas area, so returning there she made arrangements for interviews with some of the nation's best known and highly regarded companies, including AT&T, Dow Chemical, Dell Computer and Xerox. Though intriguing by name association alone, Diane concluded that were she to work for one of these corporations it is possible that she would simply become a cog in an extremely large wheel. Not that Quebecor was a small operation by any stretch, but she just sensed that the "people were somehow more real." Diane considers herself a "pretty deliberate thinker," and after weighing the true options she finally made her decision. Excited, yet apprehensive, and not altogether thrilled about moving to Boston, Diane accepted the position offered at Quebecor.

Without delay, Diane had some rather large shoes to fill. Quebecor had only hired three people directly out of college, all the other sales positions being normally filled with seasoned veterans. Not the type of woman to be frightened nor intimidated, Diane welcomed the challenge of having to prove herself to her co-workers. "In this business, especially at this company, it's really hard to just pick up the pieces, run with it and get by. You have to be very self-motivated if you want to do this. There is plenty of product knowledge offered, but little actual sales training." But she tackled the new job resolutely and the obvious results have been nothing short of amazing.

With Diane's appearance on the scene, The New England area of her profession has never been same. Landing huge accounts like Chadwick's of Boston and extending L.L. Bean's contract, Quebecor took notice of its new star. In 1992, Diane's actual gross sales topped $6 million, and in 1993 they rose above $11 million. After being named "Salesperson of the Year" in 1994, Diane stretched her sales to almost $18 million, and 1995's figures soared into the stratosphere by passing the $25 million mark. Nothing happens by chance in the business world today. Success is no accident, usually difficult to accomplish, and tough fight for most. It took hard work and hard lessons for Diane's efforts to earn the title of "amazing."

One of Diane's first discoveries was that New England is a far cry from the "friendly folks" in Dallas, and unfamiliar geography certainly had impact on her sales approach. Unlike most salespeople, Diane has never had a problem with cold calls. However, she admits that "in Texas, people are so much more friendly and inclined to talk to you and meet with you. On the East Coast, they just snap off a 'no' and hang up the phone." It was not the rejection that concerned her so much as not being given the opportunity to even make her presentations. And considering it was her job to generate new business, she was going to have to find a way to make an impact on this "East Coast attitude." "I try to create a diversion of some kind to get them to listen, and if they listen, I give them an immediate reason why they should see me." Printing is such a highly competitive industry that it's difficult to make a difference, but Diane feels if you "do a lot of homework before you make the call, you have a better shot." She believes it is imperative to know as much as you can about the client before you pick up the phone, including who they are, what they do, what their marketing needs are, and what they have done in the past. And she adds, "If you call blind, you aren't informed, and they aren't likely to give you much information."

Sales it is about information. It entails knowing price as well as manufacturing procedures, and knowing how to see into the future and anticipate how the project will develop in the long run. "These are sophisticated buyers who want an organized plan." But even the best intended of plans can be complicated. Unfortunately, Diane can propose and sell the best idea, but she has no way of ensuring its successful implementation without support and full cooperation from her manufacturing plants. Once it gets to the plant, "it's for the most part, out of my hands. I can't run the presses, I can't run the stitcher. I just have to trust them." That is the inherent problem in the industry, and that is what drives Diane to a boiling point. "For me it's errors at the printing plants. I have a really hard time accepting anything that's not perfect, and my income is dictated by how well the printing plant performs, and that's tough." Hence she has had to learn to maintain her equilibrium and build on-going relationships and depend upon production at the plants as best she can.

For someone as determined as Diane, the challenge is not to "cut off her nose to spite her face." In other words, to remain diplomatic with her manufacturing plants regardless of how frustrated she may become, and to never let the customer suffer as a result. "I have been more demanding and abrupt than I should have, but I have never lost my temper or made a blundering error with a customer." Part of the uniqueness of print sales is that the salesperson drives the project both internally and externally. They are required to apply diplomacy to every stage of the game and be politic with all parties in a cohesive way throughout the course of the sale. Diane thinks the best way to achieve that is to rely on management. "You have to coach your management. They expect you to coach them and tell them what you need from them." Having virtually no experience when she started, Diane had no choice but to look for help. "They gave me a long rope, but they were always watching the whole way and would pull me back if they saw me going down the wrong path."

The wrong path did not present itself too often. Diane is instinctively savvy, and her driving forces are a combination of keen intelligence, diligent goal setting, and mastering the art of persuasion. "My intelligence and my ability to think are my greatest strengths. With intelligence and thinking comes the ability to listen to people." Salespeople have a tendency to "babble," but Diane prefers to not only think, but "feel" while discussing specifics with her customers. She concentrates on the "big picture," and tries to rapidly formulate answers or solutions. It does not take Diane long to grasp a new idea or understand the current technologies in the industry, and she believes that those "who aren't as well-educated about the issues won't do as well. I have a hard time with ignorance." She does not consider this a fault, she just considers herself a perfectionist.

Diane is constantly striving to do the best she can for the people she works for, and part of that is generated by her ability to set her own ambitious goals. Financial goals, sales goals, any and every other kind of goal are important to her strategy for success. She overhears salespeople speak about wanting to be the best in the business, but somewhere along the line, their "desire dries up." Diane concludes that goals are the deciding factor, and they enable desire to stay fresh. "I believe everybody should set goals because it gives you something to strive for, and I believe without goals, people lose their way. They forget what they want out of life." It isn't likely that Diane will ever forget what she wants, and if you allow her to get close to those things she wants even for an instant, she just may persuade you to give it to her.

"Persuasion is the key to closing a sale." Diane is devoted to breaking down the barrier, and bringing others over to her way of thinking. Some may consider it "pushy," but if you are able to "persuade them to think about your strategy and manufacturing plan on your terms, you can get them to believe in you." Admittedly, it takes a great deal of work to persuade. It is a long arduous process to soften someone else's thinking process, but it can be done. Sometimes, however, no amount of persuasion is going to sway a customer, and that is the most tedious aspect of selling for Diane. "It's the ones you don't sell that will make you crazy because you don't really know what cost you the business." If it is not the pricing, or the manufacturing plant, the logical thought is that it has to be the salesperson, and that means somewhere the process broke down. Diane's answer is to question all of the reasons for success and failure.

"It's difficult to know from a customer's standpoint why they choose or don't choose you, so I always try to find out why." Diane strives always to improve herself and her customer relations, and if she can gain knowledge from determining the reasons for a client's decision, then she will be better prepared the next time. "I come well-armed. I ask pointed questions. I want to know what drives their decision." And when as many as six months have been invested in a single negotiation, and income is at stake, continued questions may seem somewhat strenuous. "You just have to be incredibly persistent and keep trying."

Being a woman does not dampen Diane's efforts. She has strong intentions of moving well up the corporate ladder, and is convinced that there are no "glass ceilings" at Quebecor. She even finds the gender issue to be an advantage rather than a hindrance. Printing is a male-dominated industry with male-dominated decision makers, and as sexist as it may sound, Diane's experience has confirmed her notion that "because I am a woman, a man may initially see me based on that fact alone." She does not permit it to bother her, she just wants to make a lasting impression on her company and her customers. When she first started in sales she was more concerned with monetary issues, but now Diane says the "single biggest reward is the recognition."

Being the best inevitably comes with a price. One becomes a target for others to shoot for, and the pressure can be damaging. Diane says she is "friendly with the people in her office, but I still want to be better than them." Earlier in her career, she spent a great deal of time helping others, but over time has had to shift her energies. "Any spare time I have now, I have to spend prospecting." Sales accomplishments breed stiffer competition, and Diane is careful to "watch her back." Still, knowing that she has been honored by her company as being the best in her field is motivation enough to assure continuing success.

When Diane is not at work, which isn't too often, she can be found visiting art galleries, shopping for pieces to add to her personal art collection and bouncing ideas off her new husband, Michael, who is in sales as well. And when she finally sets aside a moment or two to spend some time at home, you will find her in the kitchen. "I love to cook and have every gadget known to mankind!"

Diane Donley is uniquely destined for continued stardom. Her demeanor, her attitude, and her seemingly endless ability to generate new business will guarantee this rising star a safe and rapid flight through the constellations of Quebecor.

To Diane, the secret of success is: "Goal attainment. I am firm believer in setting goals for all aspects of your business and making yourself reach to secure them. It may take years to get there, but if you focus your efforts and develop a solid strategy you will eventually attain your goals."

• • • • • • • •

Diane Donley's personal vision of greatness:

"My vision of greatness is to add something positive to this world. Make a mark on the world, that's what I'd like to do."

Where is Diane now?

Diane is still setting and exceeding her goals at Quebecor Printing. She recently completed a multiyear deal for a whopping $40 million annually.

The Significance

"Everyone must row with the oars he has."

Egyptian proverb

The Significance

After exploring these diverse personalities, one would think it would seem fairly simple to draw concrete conclusions about the methodology of becoming a "million dollar salesperson." Nonetheless, unlocking the secret of success in sales, or any other field, is not only a very difficult endeavor, but a very personal one as well. We each measure success in our own way. Whether we use financial accomplishments, recognition, or anything else as a barometer, it is all a matter of personal perspective. The top sales performers in this book have their own unique style and characteristics and have demonstrated again and again that there are truly no set patterns to follow and no definitive answer to the question "What does it take?" Yet a few threads do run rather consistently through the impressive and complicated blanket of success.

First and foremost is perseverance - the act of persevering. The word persevere is defined by *Webster's Dictionary* as "to persist in any business or enterprise undertaken; to pursue steadily any design or course once begun; to be steadfast in purpose." Without question, perseverance is the most significant factor in the success of these salespeople. Each one of them, at some point, encountered difficulties and roadblocks to their futures. They all struggled with the choice of which direction to take their lives as well as their careers and discovered a strength within themselves that allowed them to persist in following their dreams. Perhaps their perseverance was motivated by a fear of failure, but, in the long run, it seem to be the result of the intensity of everyday hard work. And despite hardships, they never seem to have wavered from their course, their desire to be the best, and the ability to never take "no" for an answer.

Next is integrity, the quality or state of being of sound moral principle. This is another key trait that has factored into the success of these exceptional individuals. Sales and competition go hand in hand, so inevitably some salespeople may have a tendency to cross certain boundaries in regard to honesty as a means of succeeding more quickly and more profitably. Often sellers get trapped by seemingly small dishonesties that enable them to close the sale at a rapid rate, yet those dishonesties can grow and eventually they lose the long term benefits that would have resulted from an ethical transaction. This group has managed to keep their successes on an even and honest keel. They have proven that solid character is indeed an integral part of not only getting to the top, but staying at the top.

Buying and selling is a very close relationship, and these number one sellers know that building and keeping these relationships is also at the core of their successes. They all make references again and again to the "relationships" they have with their customers and the ability they have to be compassionate and "tuned in" to the customer's needs. Regardless of the always necessary give and take, there seems to be little room for selfishness if the buyer-seller relationship is to prosper. They have learned to put the customer first, address the customer's issues as a priority, and have searched to find ways to always keep the customer as happy and satisfied as possible. All of these sellers worked diligently on their business alliances and are proud to think of most all of them as friends. With these salespeople, good business relationships have become a solid foundation for their prosperity, as well as clear reflection of their own character.

Finally, and not to be forgotten, is passion. Each of these salespeople at one time saw money as a primary motivation. Eventually they discovered that there was a more important goal than how many zeros could follow a dollar sign. They found that if they loved what they were selling, believed in everything about the sale from the product to the customer, and felt passionately about their career as a whole, then the significance of financial success suddenly seemed somthing less of a burden. By being motivated by what they were doing and what they were feeling, rather than how much they could profit, the selling became more rewarding. Not minimizing the relevance of a lucrative career, they all believe that it is important not to lose sight of being satisfied with your work. Every one of them is quick to warn against the possible downfalls of using financial status as the sole measurement of success, and has fought very hard to maintain proper perspective even in the wake of their considerable earnings.

Unfortunately, there are no simple answers when it comes to successful selling. It is, however, safe to assume these individuals have all worked extremely hard for their successes, learned difficult and valuable lessons along the way, and have never lost sight of their individuality. They have had the ability to establish a selling style that works in conjunction with their own personality, and accentuates the things that they do best. There are so many ingredients that fall into the mix that it is difficult to ascertain what will and will not prove effective. But, a combination of perseverance, integrity, relationship building, and passion for your work will certainly make for a solid foundation on which to build.

About the Author

Lisa Coleman is a freelance writer in Scottsdale, Arizona. Her talents range from business writing and advertising editorial to reviewing restaurants, galleries and she was Senior Editor and Feature Writer for past issues of the Destination Arizona Book. Lisa has a Bachelor of Arts degree in English from Arizona State University. Prior to writing, she worked for ten years in government contracting and floor covering sales. Lisa is passionate about travel and spends as much time as possible discovering new places.

Order Form

To order more copies of this book, send a check for $14.95 plus $3 shipping to:

Scrivo, Inc.

7904 E. Chaparral Road, Suite A110-223

Scottsdale AZ 85250

1-800-991-1737

FAX (602) 945-2603

Total charges for book: ______________________

Shipping charges: $3 for the first book, 50¢ for each additional copy:

Total shipping charges: ______________________

TOTAL ENCLOSED ______________________

NAME: ______________________

ADDRESS: ______________________

CITY, STATE, ZIP: ______________________

Telephone #: ______________________